Welcome Carolina to South and Review Key... Thank so Much!!

To Lizzie

Wherever I traveled throughout South Carolina in my quest to produce the photography for this book, I was serenaded by the melodious mockingbird. Their cheerful song was magic on the dreariest of days. I only wish the images within these pages could be accompanied by the dazzling performance of that little creature's musical notes. You'll just have to use your imagination . . .

The photography for *South Carolina, A Scenic Discovery*, is the result of more than a year of exploration and adventure in which I had the privilege to participate. From the state's misty mountains with its deep gorges and thundering rivers to its sandy beaches and intricate marshlands with a network of twisting waterways, I am indebted to many warm and friendly folks along the way. Their helpful suggestions have been invaluable to me in producing this book. The names would fill many pages but I would especially like to thank the following people for their special efforts and Southern Hospitality: Helene Anne Ervin from Myrtle Beach; Beryl Lamotte from Hilton Head Island; Dana and Sallie Sinkler and Frances and Huger Sinkler, Jr. from Rosebank Plantation; My very special friend, canoeing companion and talented woodcarver, Granger McKoy from Wadmalaw Island; Dr. Peter and Peggy McKoy from Camden; Dottie Schipper and Ben Geer Keys from Greenville for the magic of their mountains, wildflowers and Caesar's Head. From Charleston, I am most grateful to Joseph Hanahan from Stoll's Alley for his enthusiasm, guidance and helpful contacts; And to Huger and Alida Sinkler for their help and hospitality at my wife's childhood home at 39 Church Street; To Parker and Alida Hudson, and to Frances Bonsal of Stoll's Alley; And John Kerr, my canoeing partner on the wild Chattooga. Also to all the patient pilots who got me airborne in the blackness before dawn in order to be in position for those glorious sunrises. And to Nikon for their dependable cameras and lenses from which all the Kodachrome 64 film was shot.

I am fortunate indeed to know all these wonderful folks from South Carolina, none of which would have been possible without an introduction from my wife, Elizabeth, daughter of Frances Marshall Canfield of Charleston. It is with a great deal of love that I dedicate this book to my wife, Elizabeth Bigelow Canfield Smith.

Clyde H. Smith

Overleaf: Live oaks and Spanish moss

Copyright ©1984 Foremost Publishers, Inc.
All rights reserved.
This book, or portions thereof, may not be reproduced in any form without permission of Foremost Publishers, Inc.
Edited by James B. Patrick.
Designed by Donald G. Paulhus.
Printed in Japan.
ISBN 0-89909-048-6

Published by Foremost Publishers, Inc.
An affiliate of Yankee Publishing Inc.
Durham, New Hampshire 03444

SOUTH CAROLINA
A Scenic Discovery

Photography by Clyde H. Smith, Introduction by William Price Fox

Published by Foremost Publishers, Inc.
An affiliate of Yankee Publishing Inc.

It could have been, it should have been, it was.

My dad, who spent some time in Europe during WWII and who could tell a story with the best of them, had his own theory about why South Carolina is so different. When he was in Palermo he saw a painting of St. George slaying the dragon in which St. George was about six feet tall and built like a wide receiver. The dragon came in at 80 hands high, weighing over 50 tons and throwing out a 60-foot sheet of blue-red flame. Dad said that as he traveled through north into Italy he kept seeing the same painting but while George stayed about the same size, the dragon kept getting smaller. In Germany he was down to the size of a Clydesdale and still shrinking. Finally, in Copenhagen, he said he couldn't believe it. "That dragon still looked like a dragon, but the artist had shrunk him down to the size of a good-sized rabbit. Old George was holding him up by one ear. I mean, he couldn't have dressed out no more than four pounds tops." Then he summed it all up. "The way I see it, South Carolina is about like Palermo: we have more imagination down here and, you know, bigger visions."

We also have the Gullah dialect, which centers around Charleston and the low country. Down there they read heads and work roots. They believe that "haint blue and haint green" painted on the door jambs and window trim will keep the evil spirits away, and that if you sweep your yard before the sun comes up, Doctor Death will keep on the other side of the road. In Gullah, "he" stands for he, she, or it, and "um" stands for it, her, him or them. Many of the words and phrases run on pure sound and cadence; if it sounds good, it is good. Proper names can be name brands, roads signs, or anything that comes down the pike. One woman near Beaufort, who was named during the Kennedy funeral, proudly displays Cathedral Rotunda Johnson on her RFD mailbox. And over near Fripp Island, the town of Pocataligo is the compression of "poke a turtle's tail and he will go." Of the translatable Gullah proverbs, here are three: "Ef you play wid puppy, ee lick you face" (familiarity breeds contempt); "Ef you ent hab hoss to ride, ride cow" (half a loaf is better than none"; and "Po buckra an dog walk one pat" (the poor man and the dog walk the same path).

On East Bay Street in Charleston, the oldest printers in the south, Walker, Evans and Cogswell, knowing the precarious ways of the American dollar, still hold on to their original confederate money plates. Charlestonians hold on to anything old: their houses, their furniture, their she-crab soup recipes and their accents. It's this "holding-on" to the best things of the past and its sacred belief in landmarks that make Charleston possibly the most beautiful city in the country. With the low skyline and gas lantern-lit cobblestone streets you can stroll along at night with a good domestic wine and be in southern France, or Kerry County, Ireland, or back on the pages of Jane Austen. Charlestonians also — despite earthquakes, hurricanes and outright ridicule — cling to their family names with a desperation that approaches the American Kennel Club. If a young married lady is introducing herself she might admit that she is now unfortunately a Hampton: "I'm Elizabeth Moultrie Hampton." Then, with a perfectly sensible "south of Broad Street" change of key, she'll quickly add, "wuzza Heyward."

   May is too late for azaleas and too early for crepe myrtle, but the magnolias are as wide as your two hands and the gardenias and mimosa are out and it's the perfect time for Spoleto, the International Music Festival in Charleston which features opera, ballet, chamber music, theatre, everything. I remember one year when the centerpiece for the jazz portion was Ella Fitzgerald. Her stage was the Cistern at the College of Charleston where over 200 years ago they trapped the rainwater for drinking water. Out under the Spanish moss-draped live oaks, it was one of those great nights to remember. The stage lights were bouncing off the low clouds and splashing on the cymbals and the big Steinway piano, where Art Flanagan played and led Ella back over her old but still brand new trails. Couples carrying wine and six packs of beer had climbed up into the low limbs of the spreading oaks, which almost covered the stage, and an orange-red moon was rising. Ella's first song, "Do Nothing Till You Hear From Me," was absolutely perfect and absolutely no one else's. She sang another and then another and the beautiful night rolled on. On her last number as she snapped her fingers into an old rhythm, the moon, which had turned silver, suddenly, as if on cue, came down the open shafts of the Spanish moss. For a lot of us out there under the stars, we knew that some things resist time and the tides and the affairs of man. It could have been ten years ago, twenty years ago, thirty, but we also secretly knew it could have only happened here in Charleston.

I grew up in Columbia, and every day on the way to school I could see the green-domed State House with its bronze stars on the western side marking the spots where Sherman's shells had struck. They are still there and will probably remain there forever. We were all raised and educated with the same set of unassailable facts: William Tecumseh Sherman was the goateed devil; Lincoln was acceptable because of his Kentucky birth but confused because of his poor marriage; Ulysses S. Grant was a heavy boozing atheist. Robert E. Lee and Stonewall Jackson and Jeb Stuart were our gods, and the local historians took a liberal poetic license to make sure they stayed that way. We grew up with history all around us. In the old section of town the streets are named for the Revolutionary generals: Bull, Sumter, Marion. In the newer section, they bear the names of the Confederate leaders: Lee, Jackson, Pickett and Greene. And in the section called the Bottom, the street names are for comic book characters, boxers, attitudes, and ambitions: Do Rite Alley, Easy Street, Sugar Ray Robinson Blvd., and Captain Marvel Road — which is ten feet from the railroad tracks and dead ends at a trash pile.

In the small towns around Greenville, Florence, Aiken and Columbia some things never change. The

Atlantic Coast Line and the Southern tracks still gleam in the white gravel and the bright sun. Dogs still follow kids to school and wait outside under the chinaberry trees, and cats still cool themselves under the houses up against the chimney bricks, and Fords and Chevys and Plymouths still rust and rot out in the front yards and down in the drain ditch. Around Columbia we grew up shooting squirrels in the swamp and carp in the river and rats at the trash pile. We sold iron to the iron man, paper to the paper man, and whiskey bottles to the bootleggers, and rode our bikes down the fifty or sixty steps of the State House. And later, after the bikes, there were cars. And during the cars there was Carlyle Miller, who spent every waking minute waxing and polishing his Dodge. He'd Simonize it, dry-rub it, wet-rub it, spit-rub it, and buff and chamois it until it was too dark to see and still it was never right. And we'd ask him, "Hey, Carlyle, when you taking old Bobbie Lee out?" Carlyle would look thoughtful and, folding his chamois cloth up as if it was a silk handkerchief, say "Soon as I get some new seat covers." He'd get new seat covers. "How about it now, Carlyle?" "Pretty soon now. All I need me is some hub caps." New hub caps would glisten on Carlyle's gleaming Dodge. "Now Carlyle?" "Almost ready. Thought I'd pick up some mud flaps." "Yeah, that would be pretty slick."

Red rhinestones on the mud flaps, raccoon tails trailing from the parking light, the antennae, the bumper guards, a ruby knob on the gear shift, and Mexican ball fringe around the back window ledge, the front dash and framing the rear view mirror, and finally, when there was nothing else to buy, or place to put it, or nothing to shine, tune up, tighten, or smooth out, and Carlyle had painted himself into a corner, he stepped neatly out of it by selling the Dodge and buying a Harley Davidson with a single seat.

    South Carolina with its own language, its own stories and its own rhythms is different, very different. You'll see glimpses of it in the shrimp boats and the oyster boats heading out at dawn and coming back in at dusk. In the giant blue heron as it glides across a marsh or when a possum (the small dog who does not bark) crosses a road carrying her litter and in that soft and sliding light at first dark that turns the roofs of Charleston from red to orange to gold to umber. My dad was probably right: if we're like anyone, we're like Palermo because while we know much of what we carry on about doesn't make sense, we believe it anyway. We have our own vision and version of history which runs: it could have been, it should have been, it was. And in this happy delusion sustained by December roses and gardenias and dollar-a-pound-shrimp and weather you can play golf in almost every day of the year, we still believe that if Robert E. Lee had had Stonewall Jackson on his flank at Gettysburg we would have won the day and the war, and the capitol of these United States would be dead between Greenville 100 miles north and Charleston 100 miles south, right here in Columbia, where it was originally scheduled to be.

                                            William Price Fox

One of 300 sculptures in Brookgreen Gardens

The jasmine, state flower

Rosebank Plantation on Bohicket Creek, Wadmalaw Island.

Burt Stark House, Abbeville

Dogwoods blooming in Pendleton

Sunrise beyond the mountains

Lace House, Columbia

Easter egg hunt in Stoll's Alley, Charleston   *Overleaf:* Middleton Gardens flowering peach

Early Fall colors under Table Rock

Confederate memorial and state offices, Columbia

Shrimp boat rounding Bird Key at sunrise   Colonial Lake shoreline, Charleston

Stoll's Alley house, Charleston

Gleaming reminders of gracious living *Overleaf:* Reservoir under Table Rock

Bull Island beach

"Frog Baby" fountain at Brookgreen Gardens

Stately columns of Charleston

A breathless moment on Table Rock

Early crossing of Lake Keowee on SC11   *Overleaf:* Kudzu conquers all

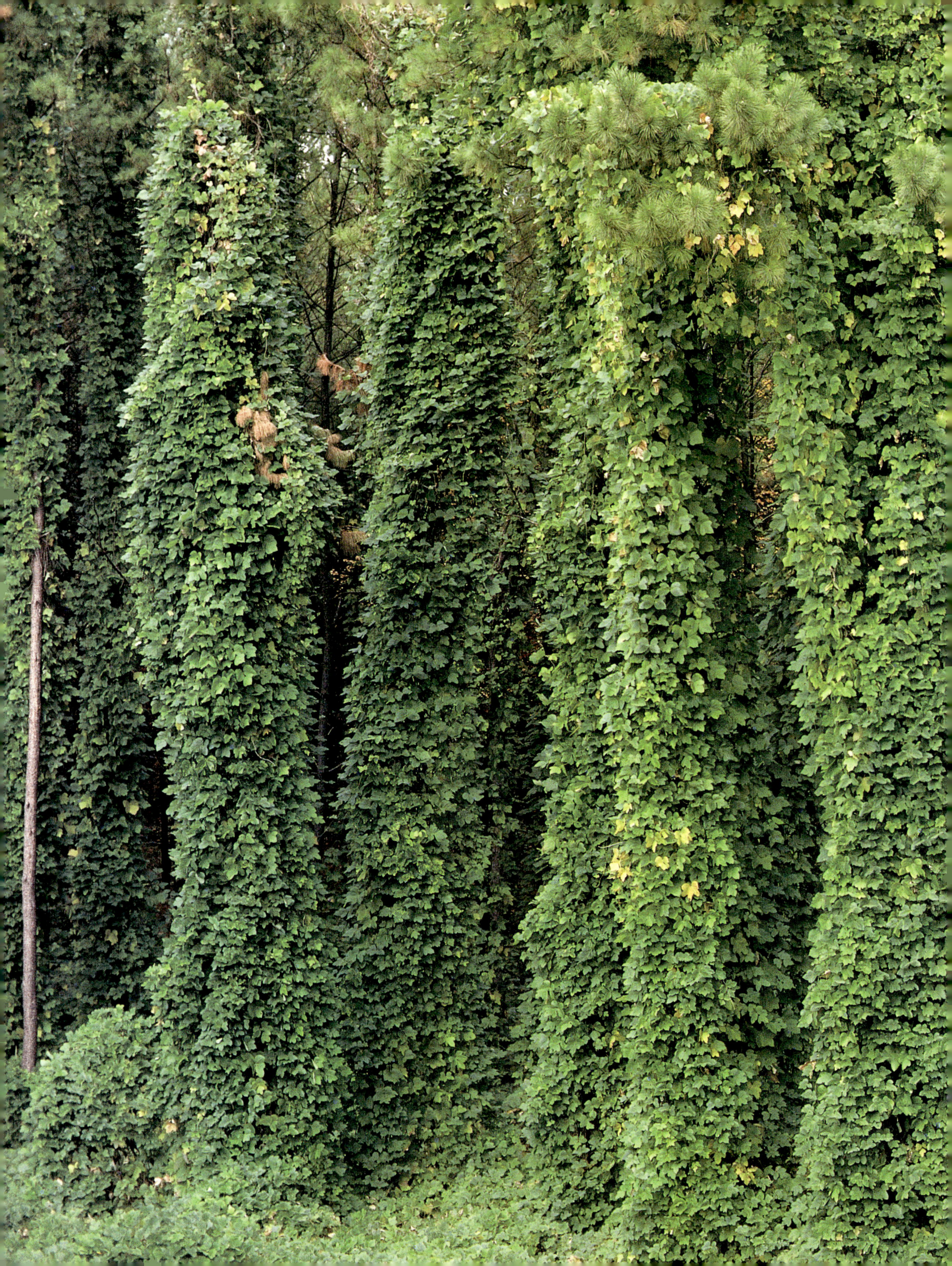

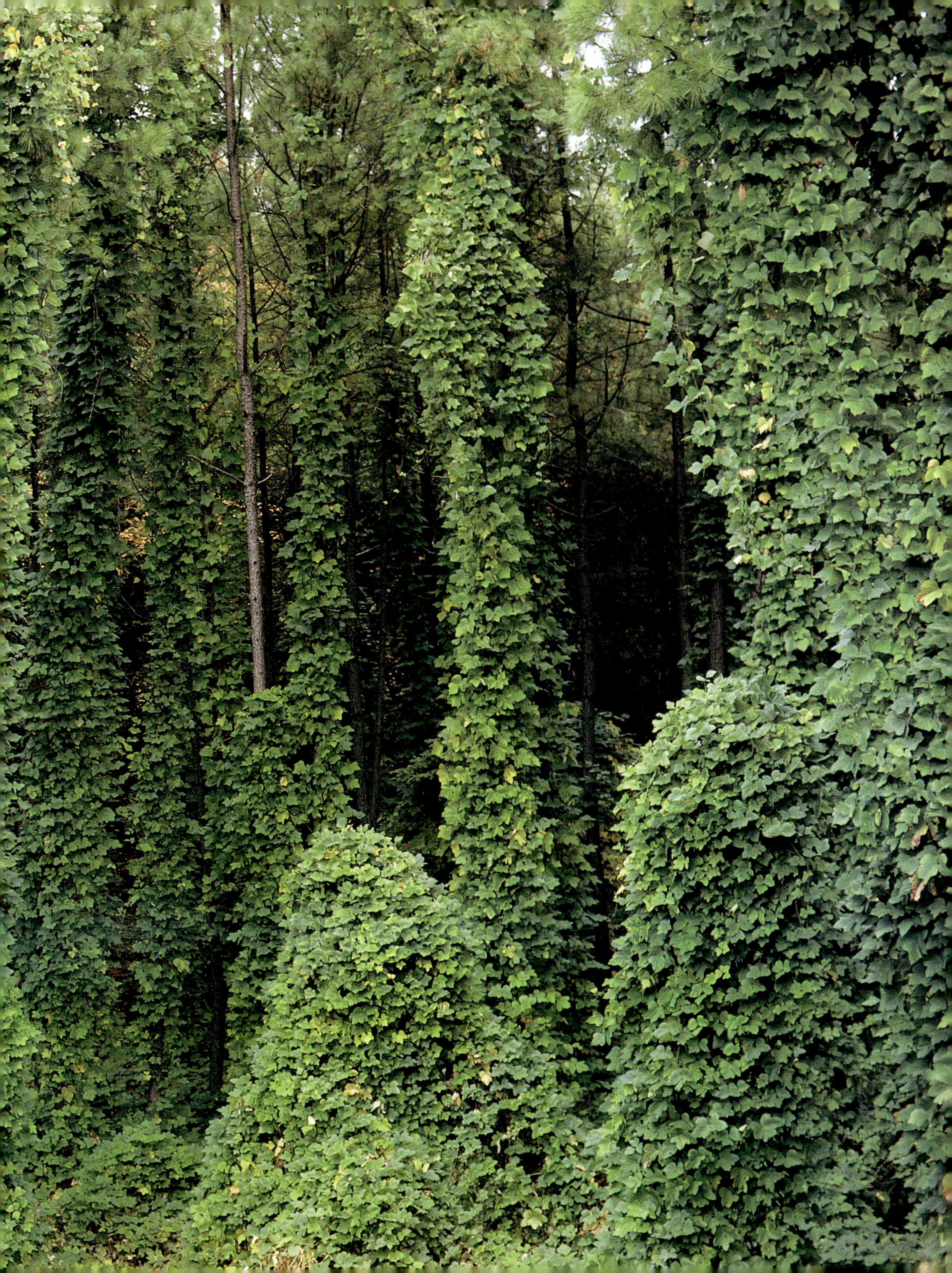

Newry on Lake Keowee

Cape Romaine National Wildlife Refuge

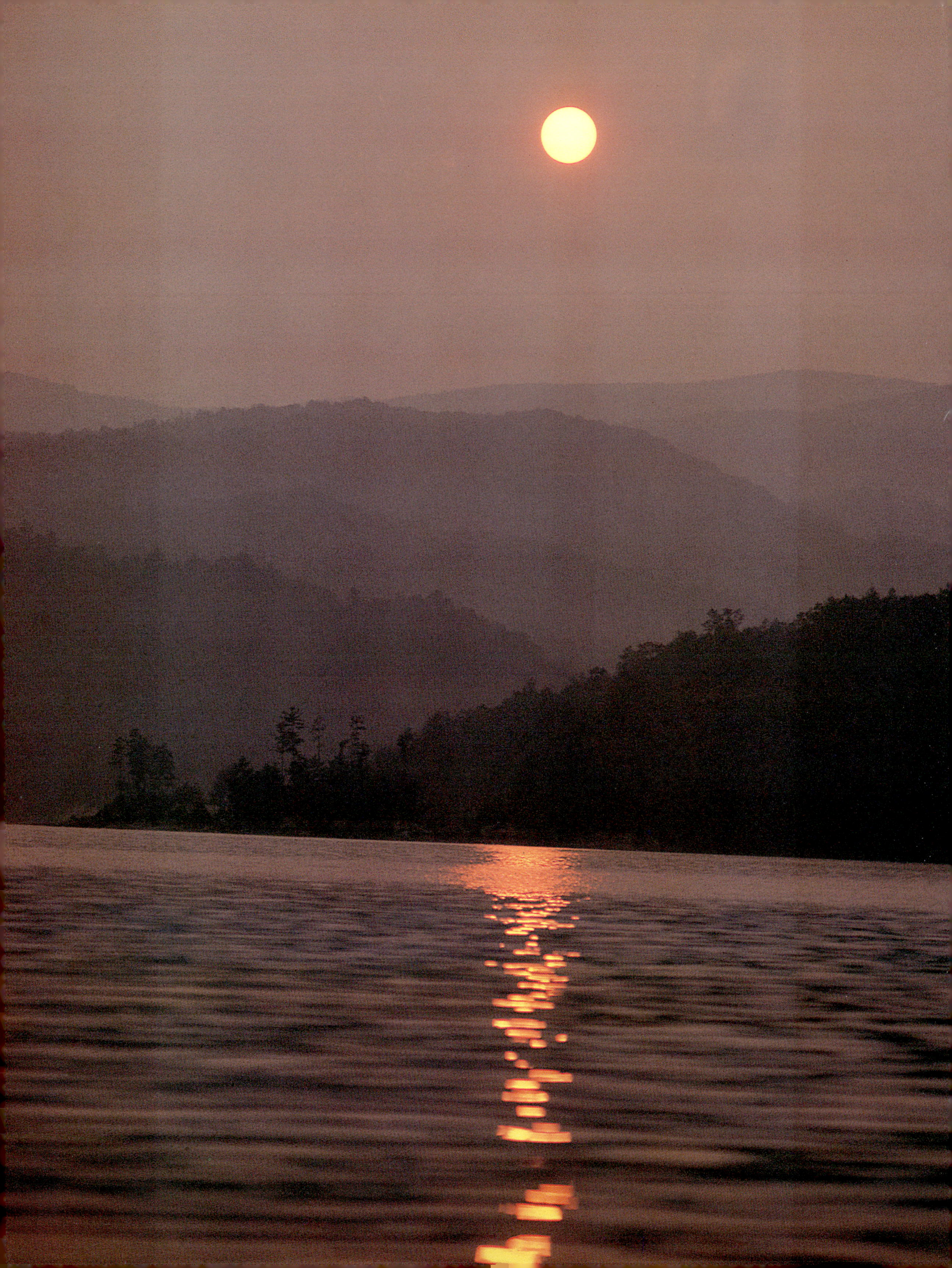

Lake Jocassee at sunset

Medway Plantation

Raven Cliff Falls

Canoeing the Chatooga   *Overleaf:* Harbor Town at Hilton Head

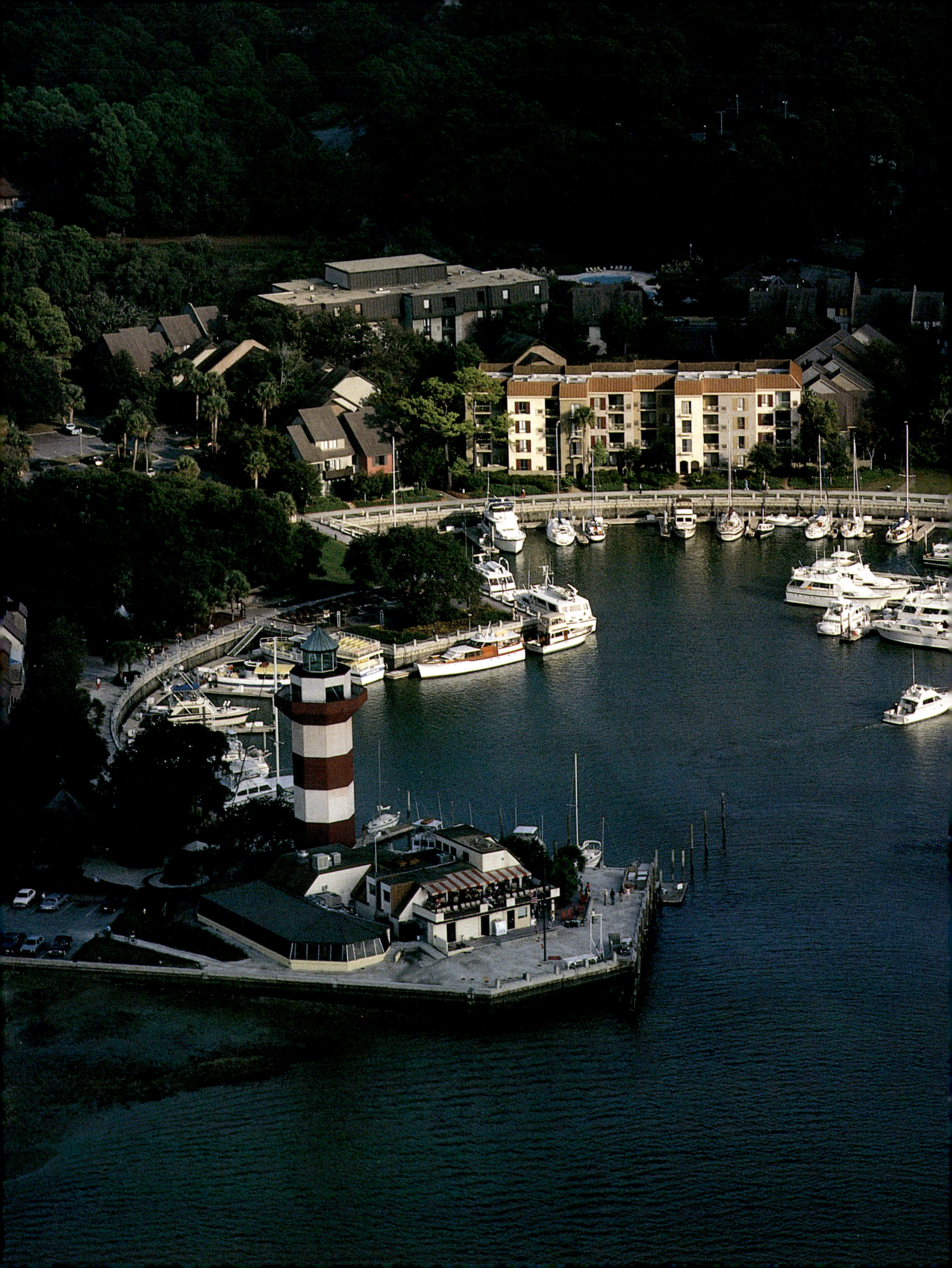

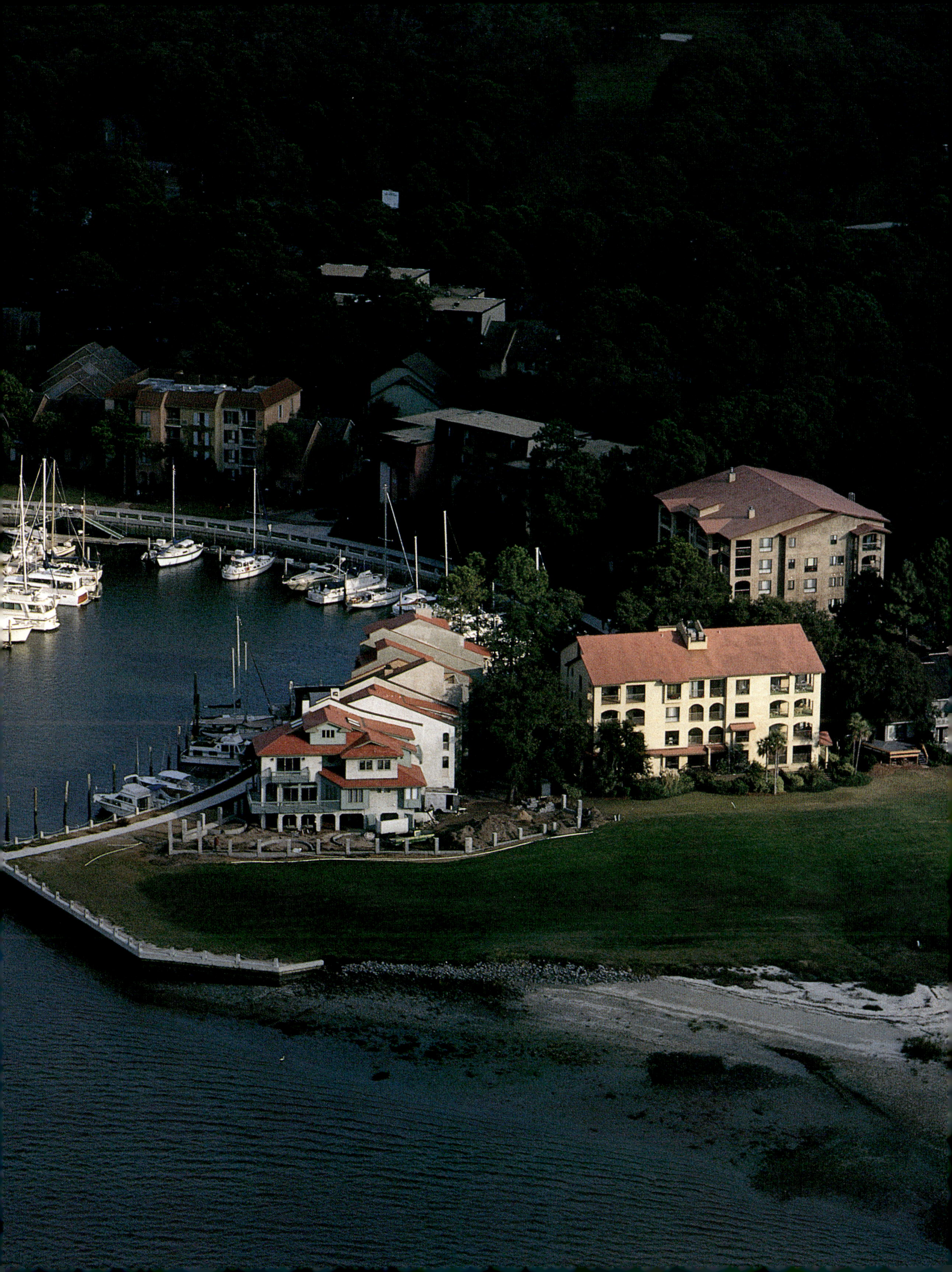

St. Philip's, Sr. Michael's and Ashley River, Charleston

Refreshment time before a Battery house, Charleston

Furman University, Greenville

Kiawah Island ribbon

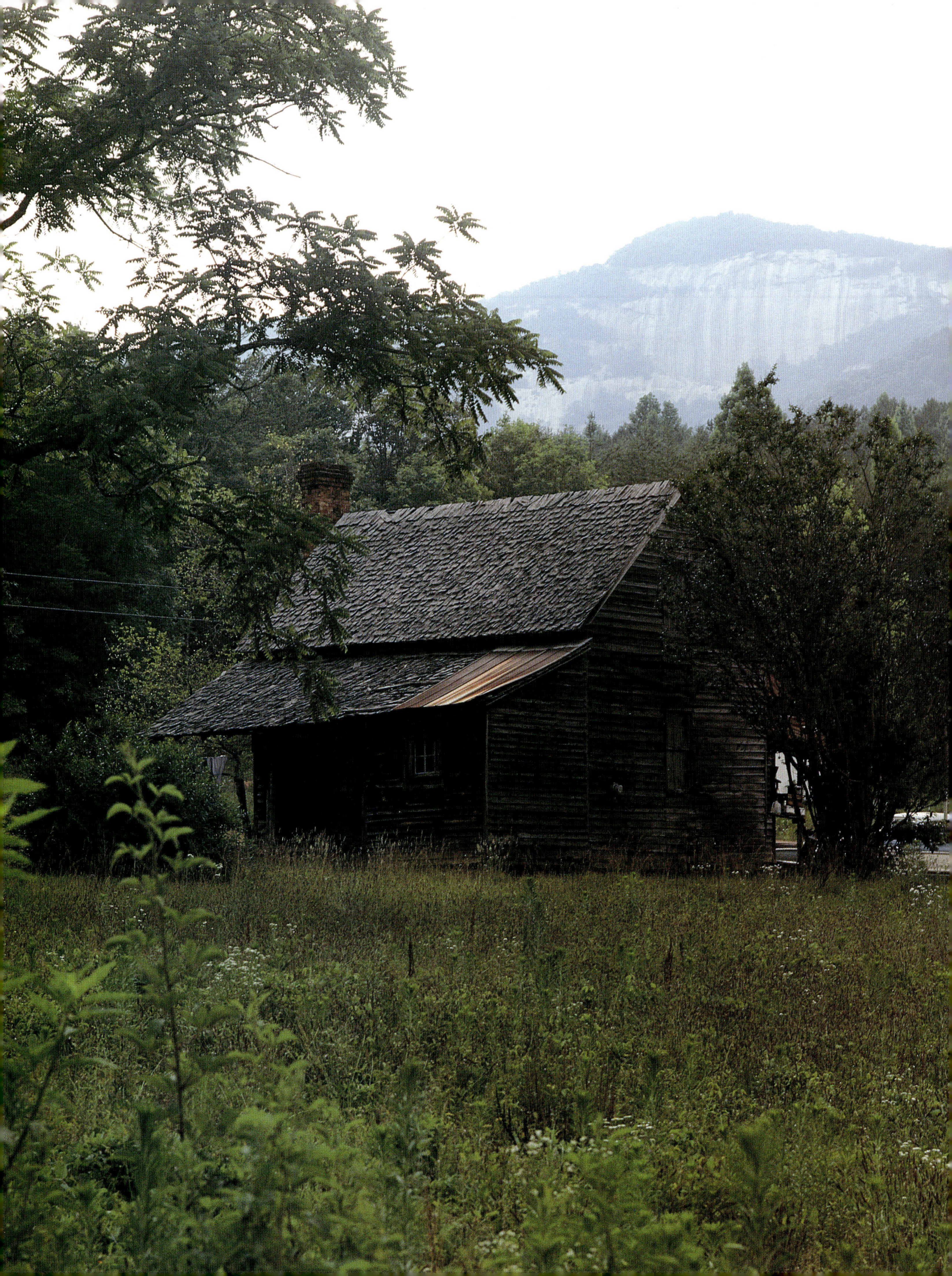

Cabin in the mountains .... Elbert Brown, basketmaker – age 90, Pendleton 51

Governor's mansion, Columbia

Foal follows mare in River Falls Valley   *Overleaf:* View from Sassafras Mountain

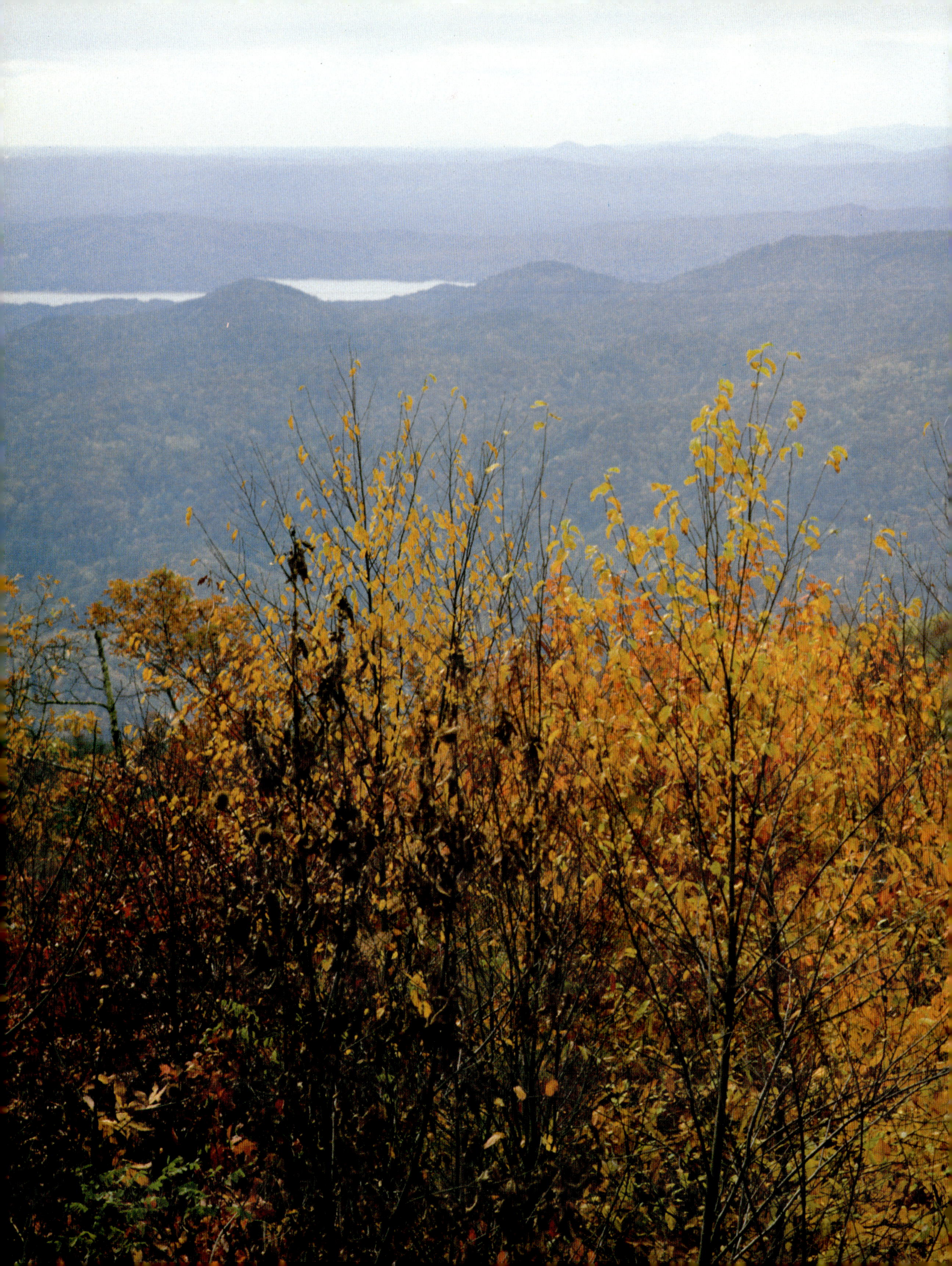

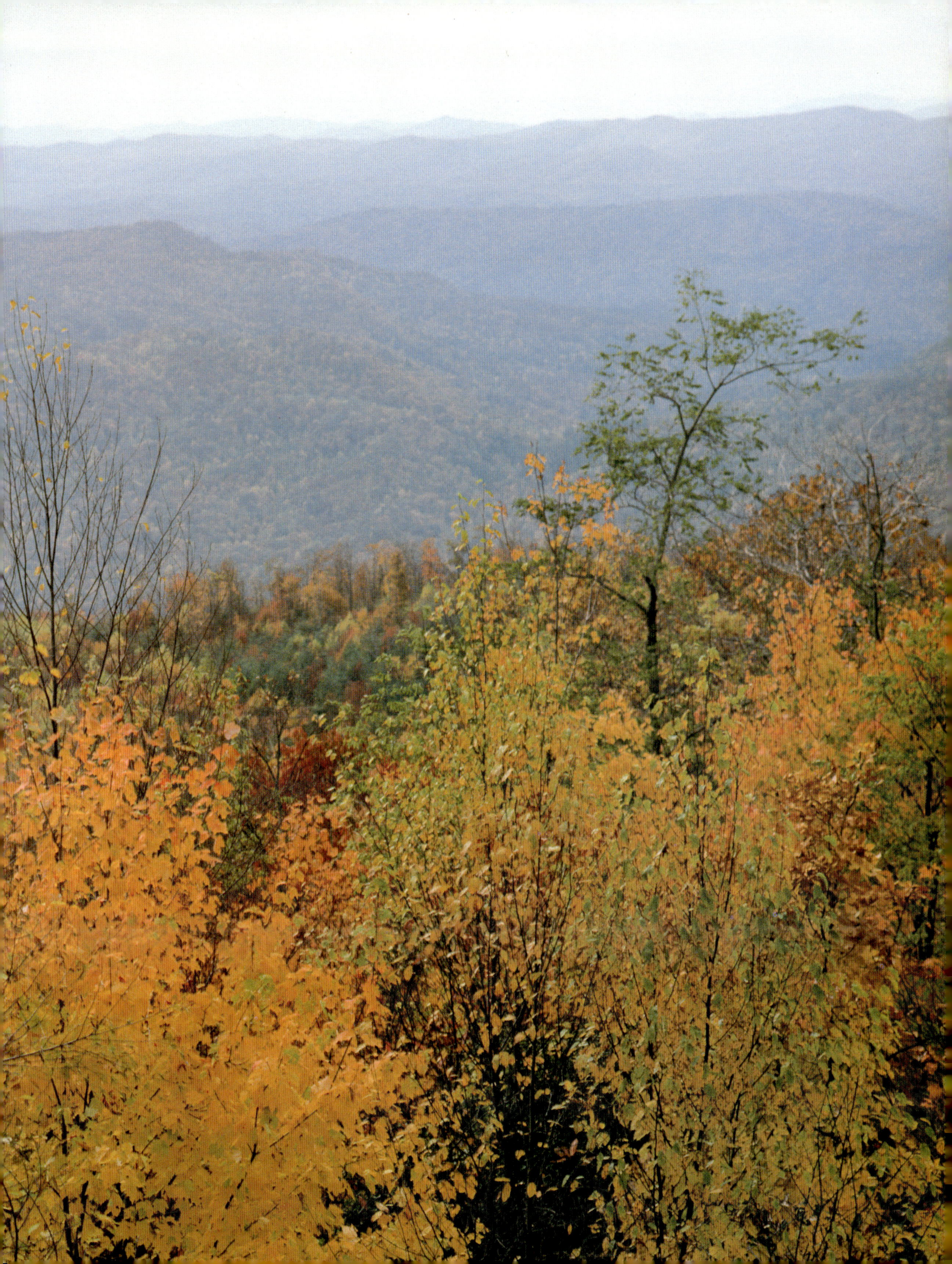

Grass of Parnassus

Egret emerging

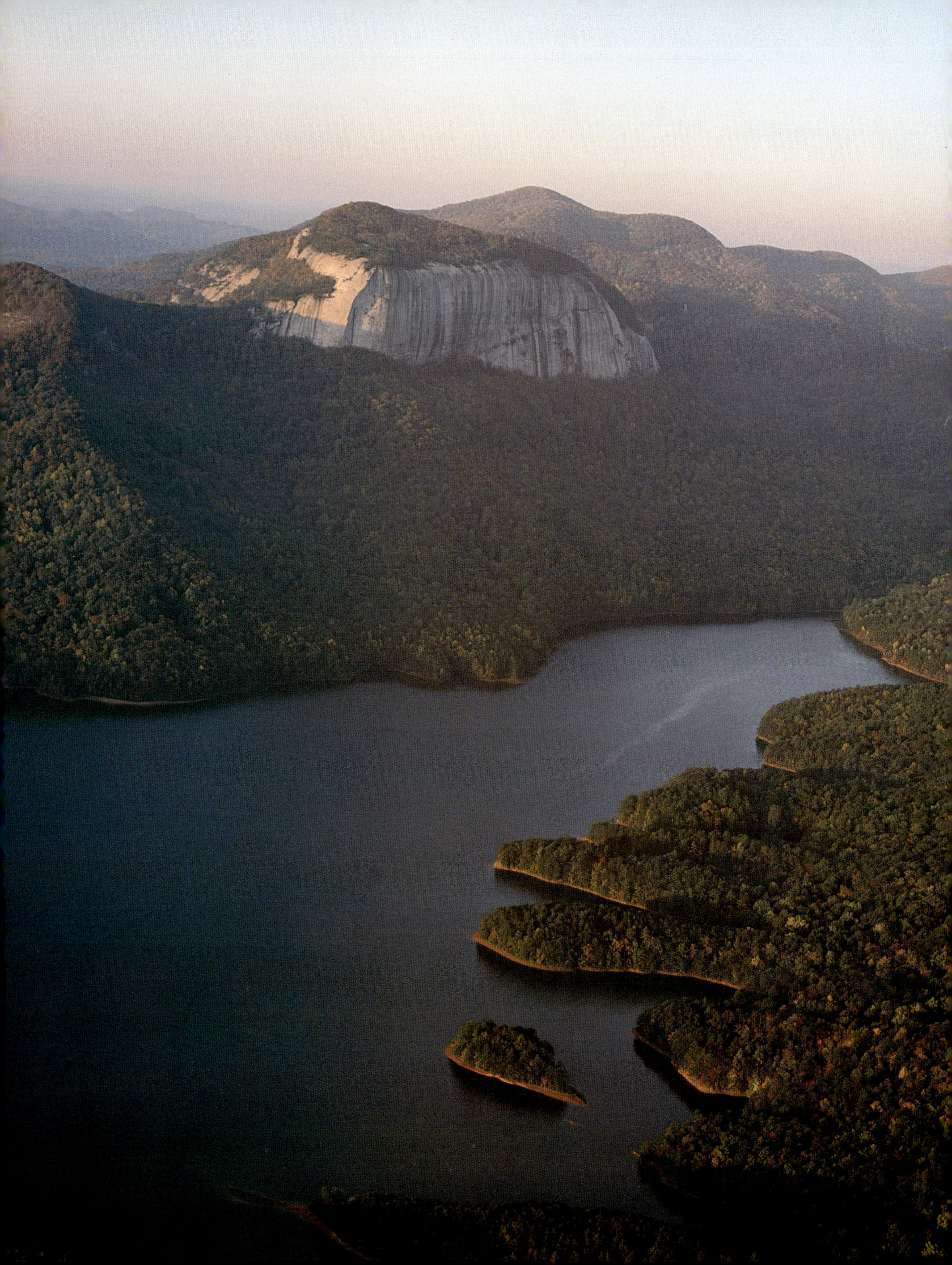

Greenville Reservoir and Table Rock　　　　　　The city of Greenville

A football afternoon at Clemson

The marching brass of Clemson   *Overleaf:* Church spire reaches for Table Rock

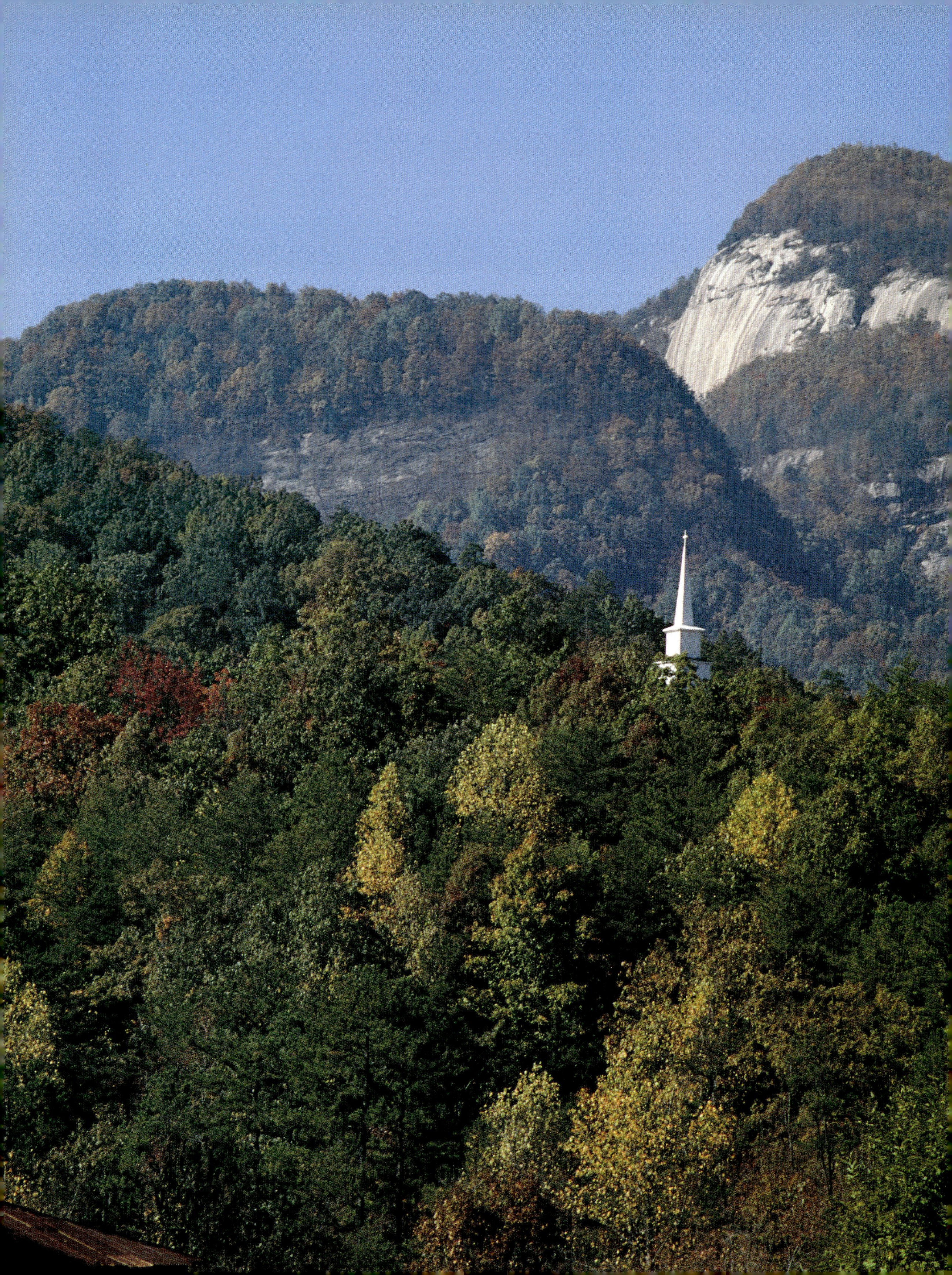

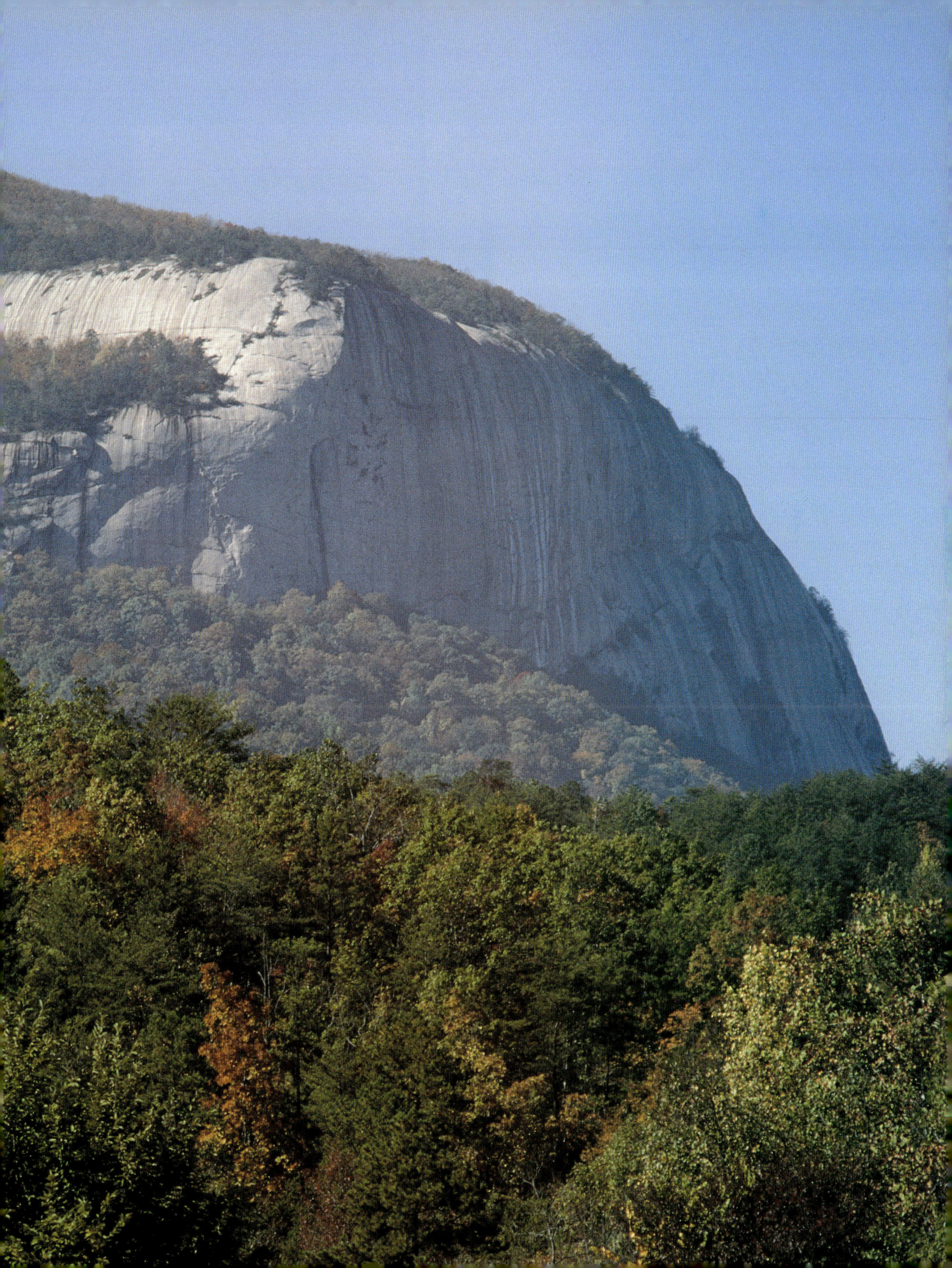

Dawn on Bohicket Creek, Wadmalaw Island

Alligator country

Dogwood blossom

College of Charleston, founded 1770

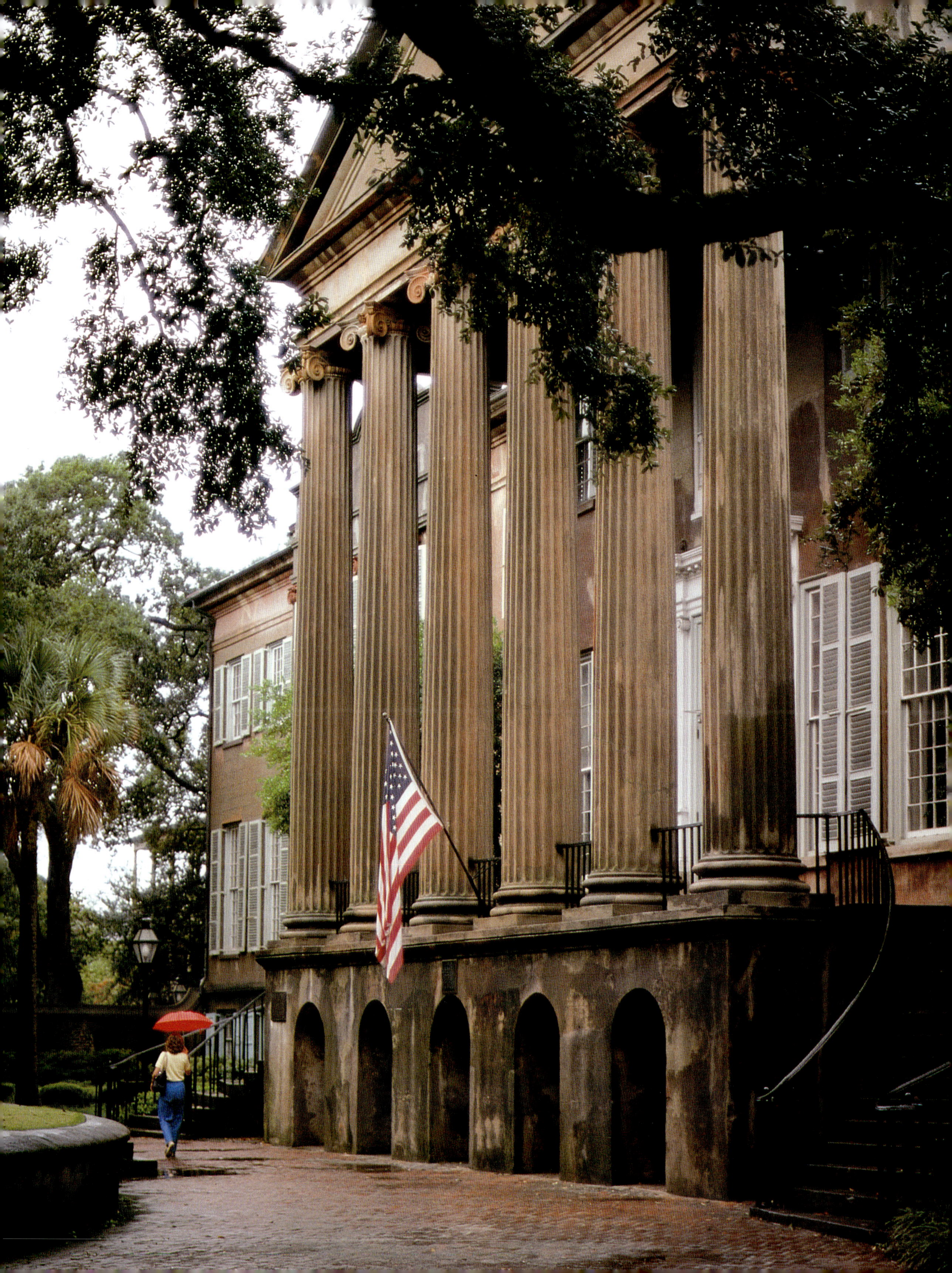

Flea market seller at Pickens

Flea market buyers at Pickens

Cypress water is otter country

Fall Creek Mill near Chatooga River Gorge

Aiken stable

Beaufort home   *Overleaf:* Middleton Gardens in bloom

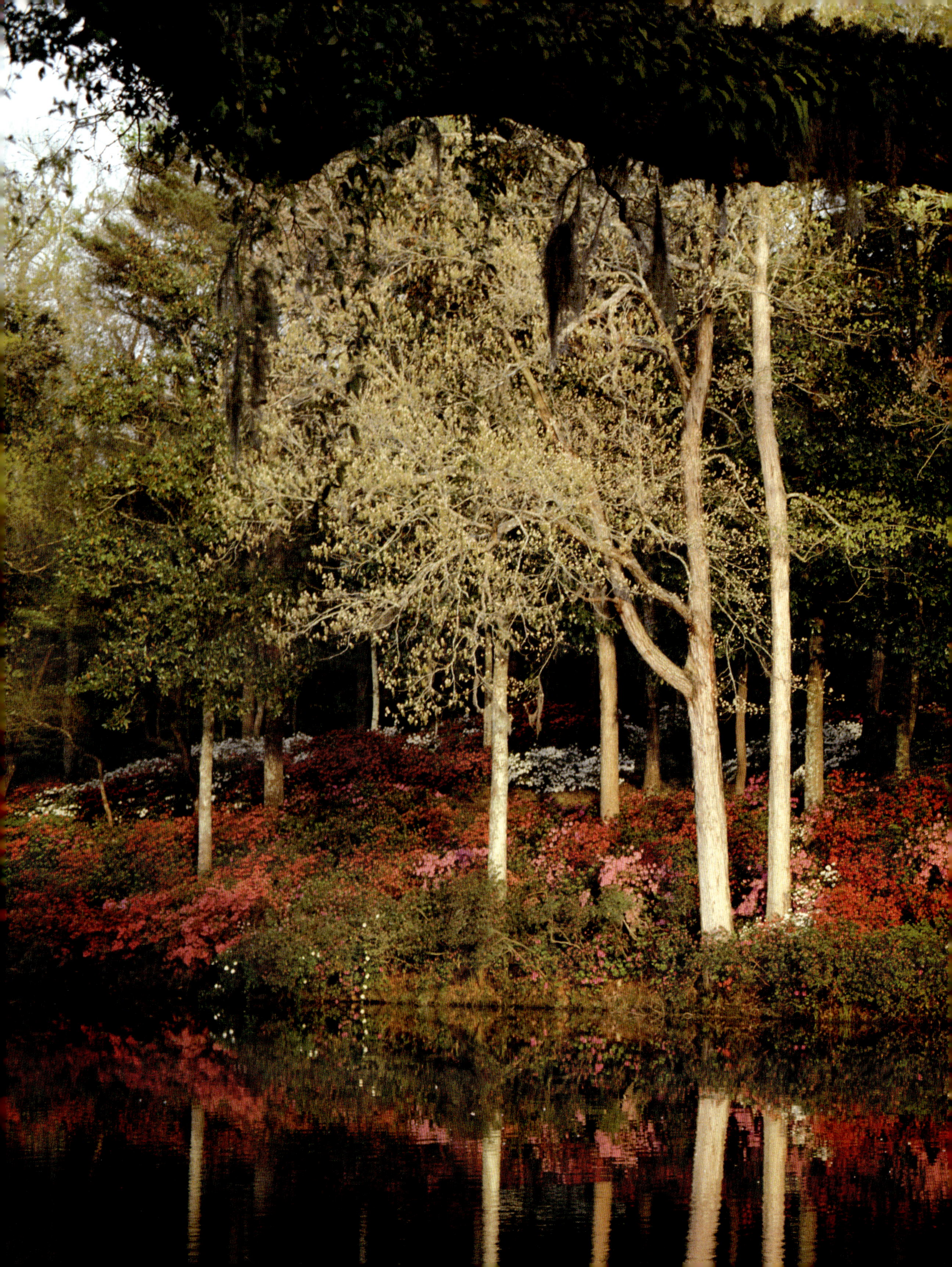

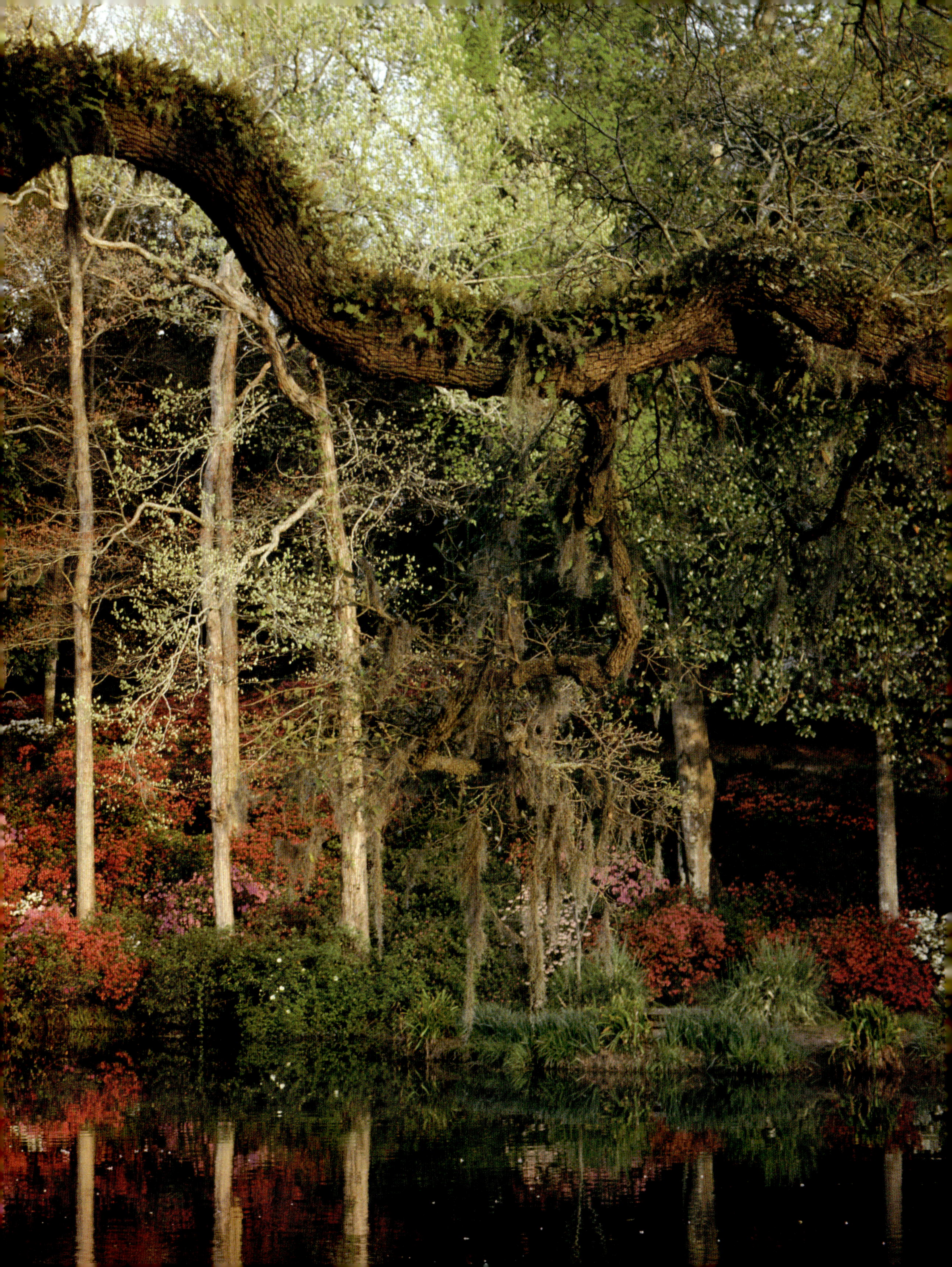

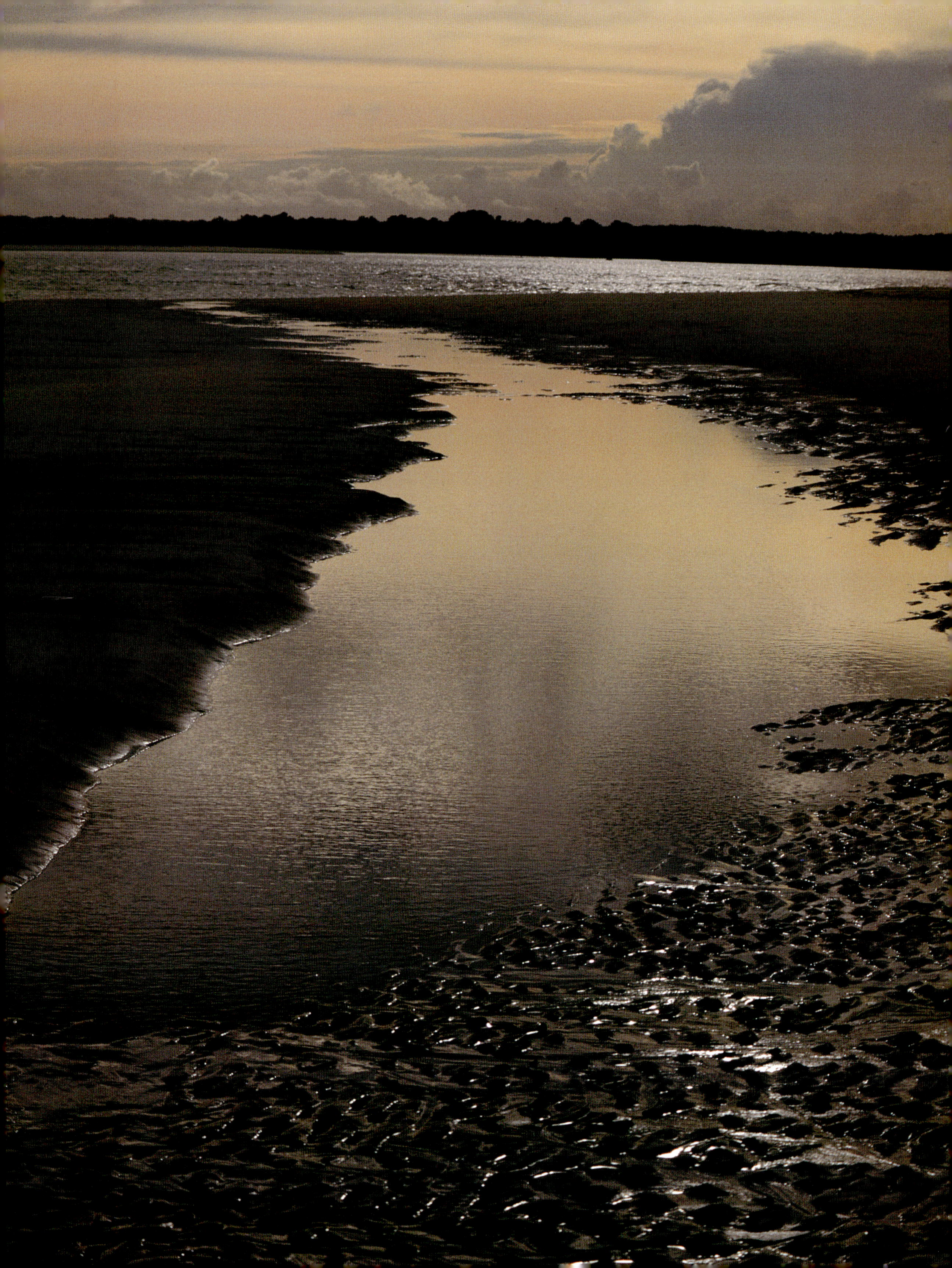

Myrtle Beach   Crabs at low tide.   77

Cadets at The Citadel, Charleston

Chapel flags at The Citadel

Myrtle Beach State Park fishing pier

Sandpipers   *Overleaf:* Patterns on Bull Island

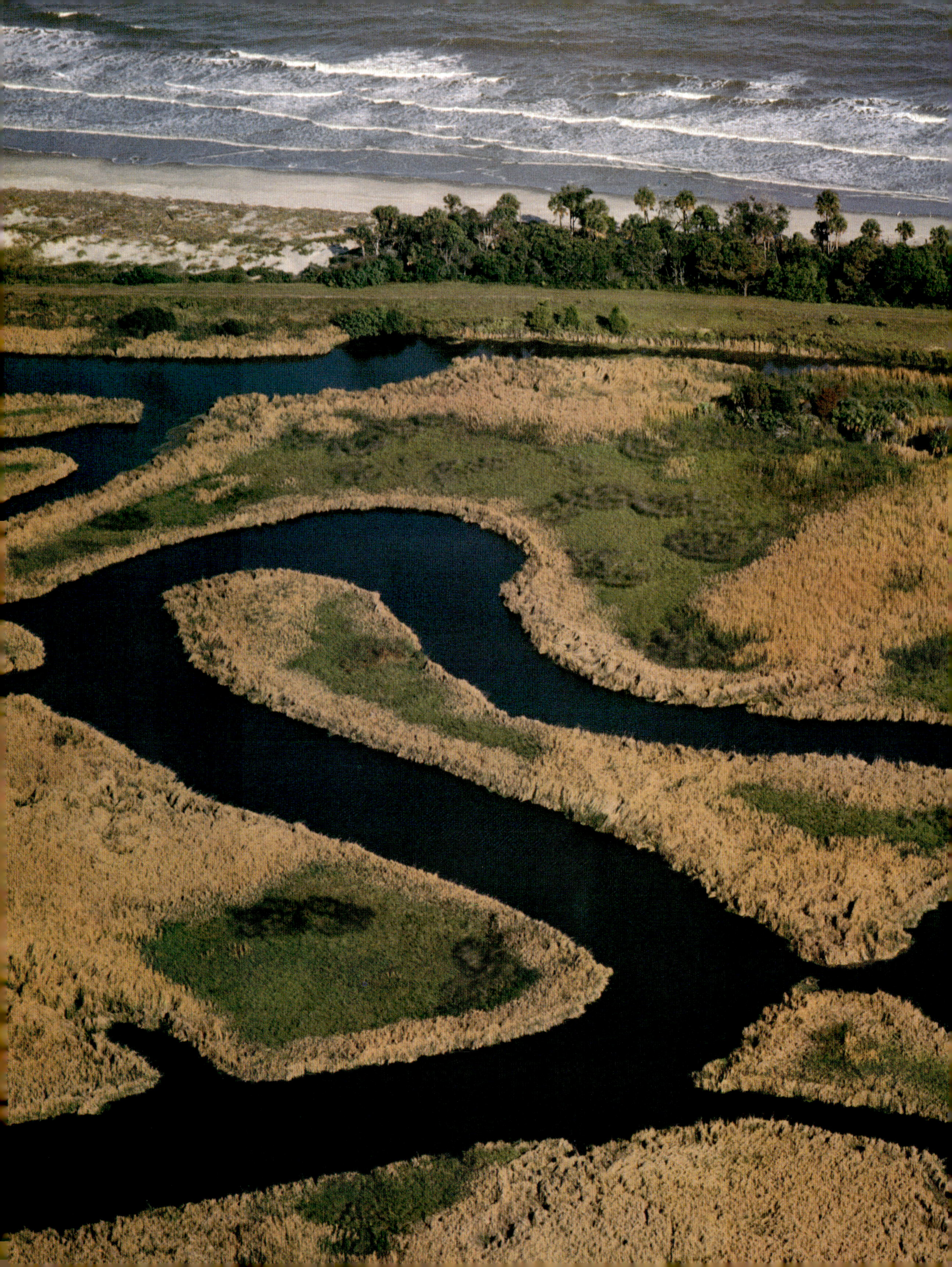

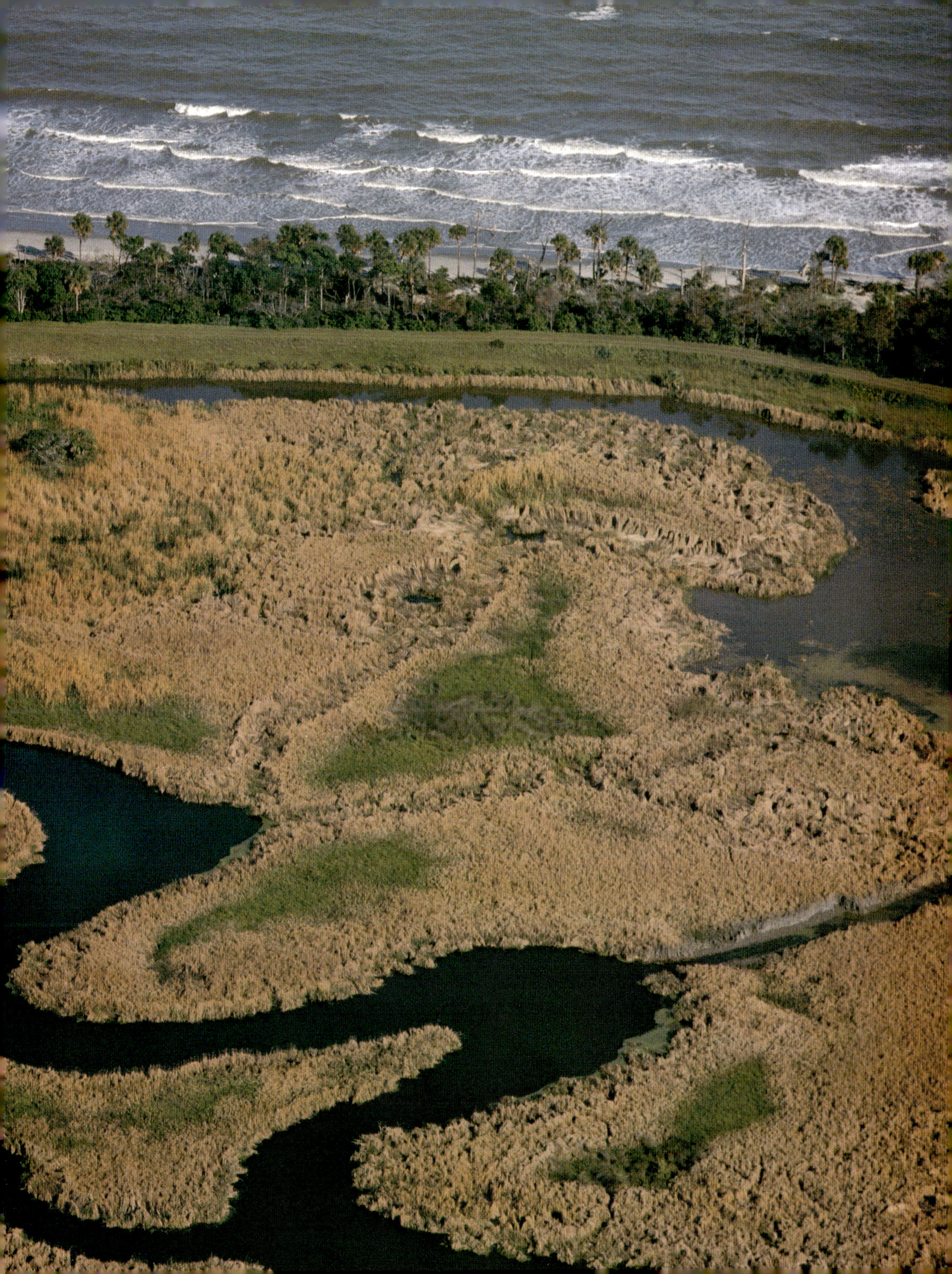

Old Indian Mountain

St. James Santee Episcopal Church, McClellanville

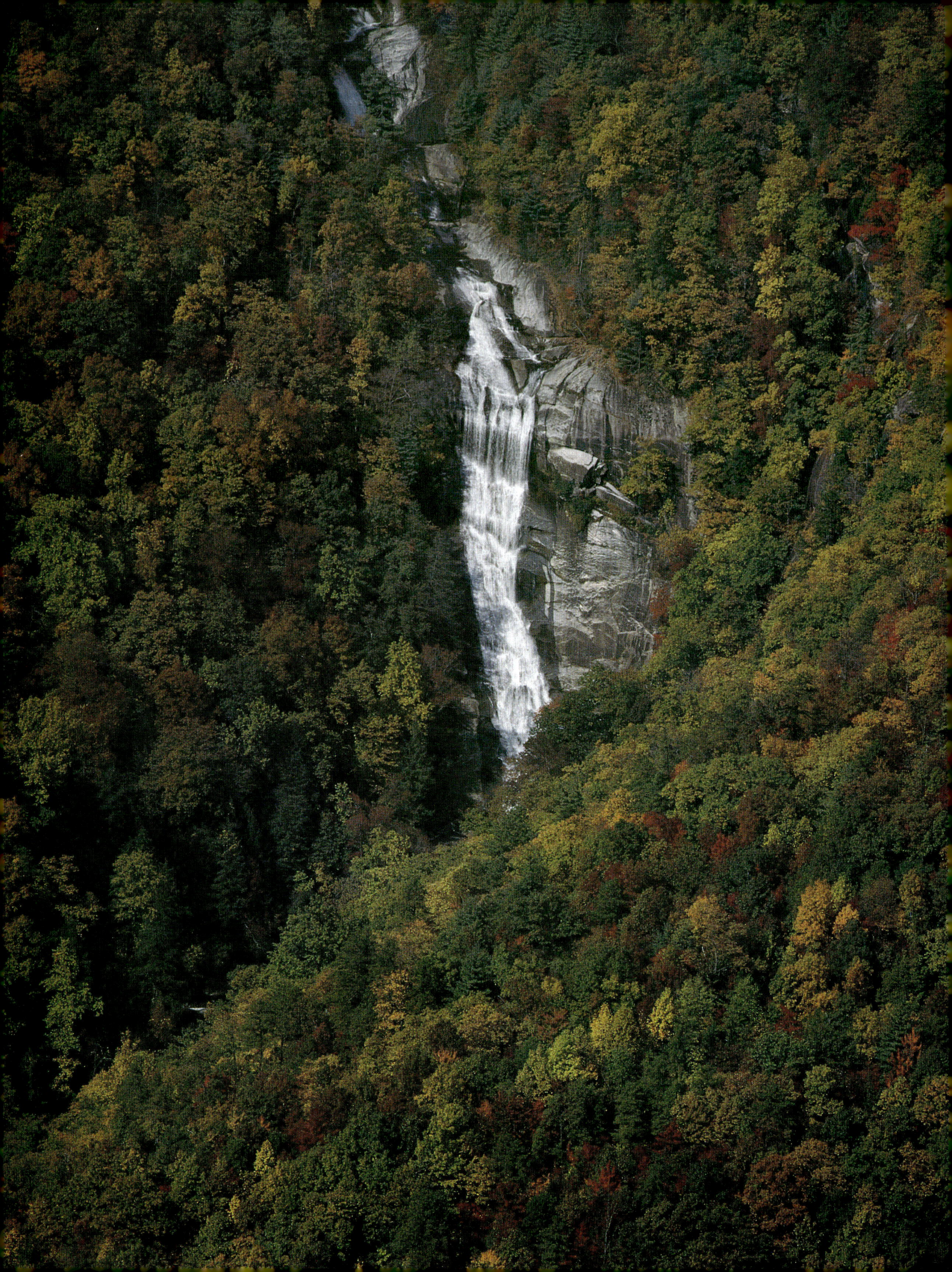

Whitewater Falls above Lake Jocassee   Shooting Bull Sluice on the Chattooga River

Egrets and herons roost on a live oak

Cypress Gardens

"How beautiful upon the mountains" – Symm's Chapel

Ripples at sunset in Murrill's Inlet   *Overleaf:* Sand and sky at Murrill's Inlet

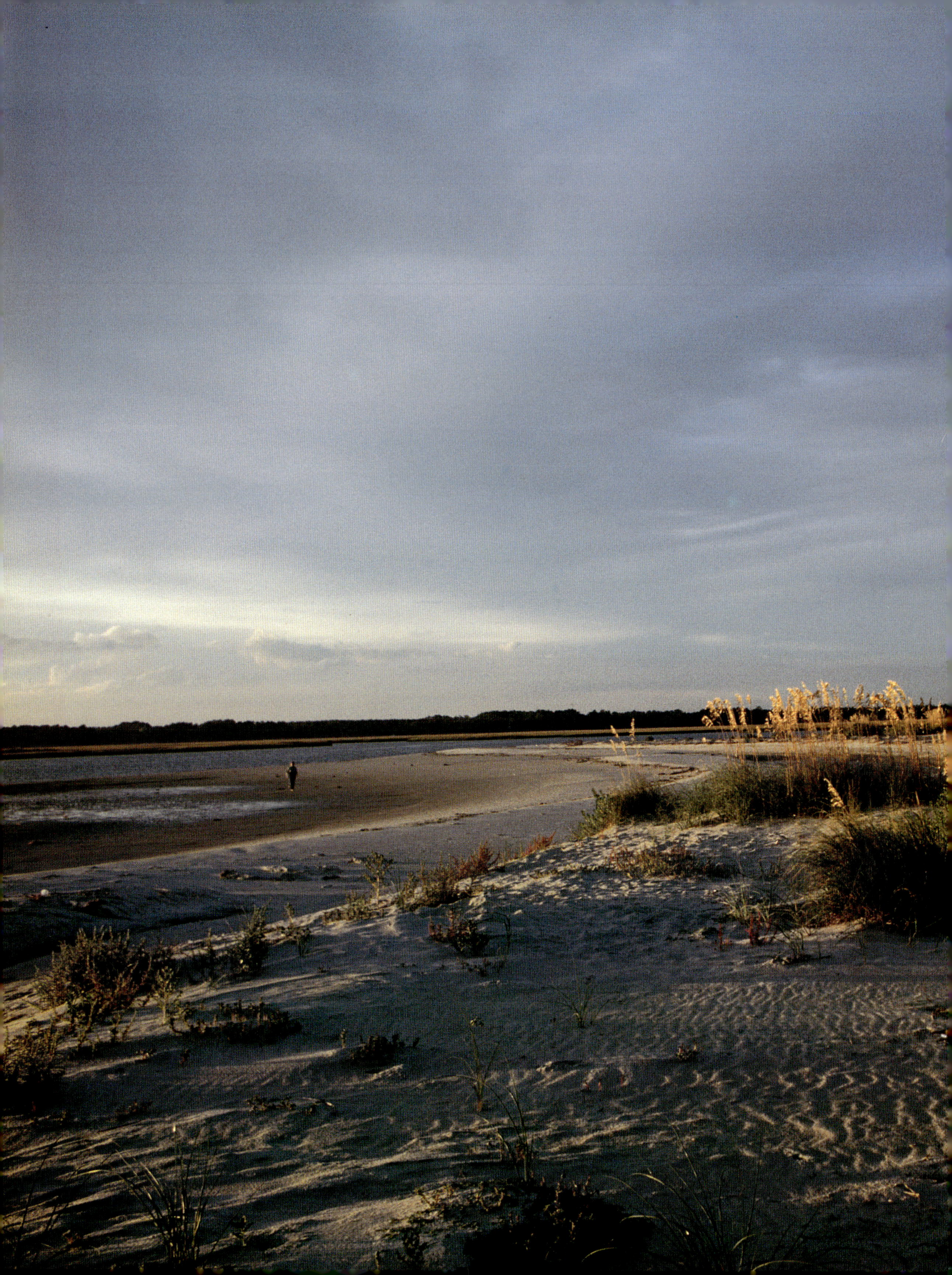

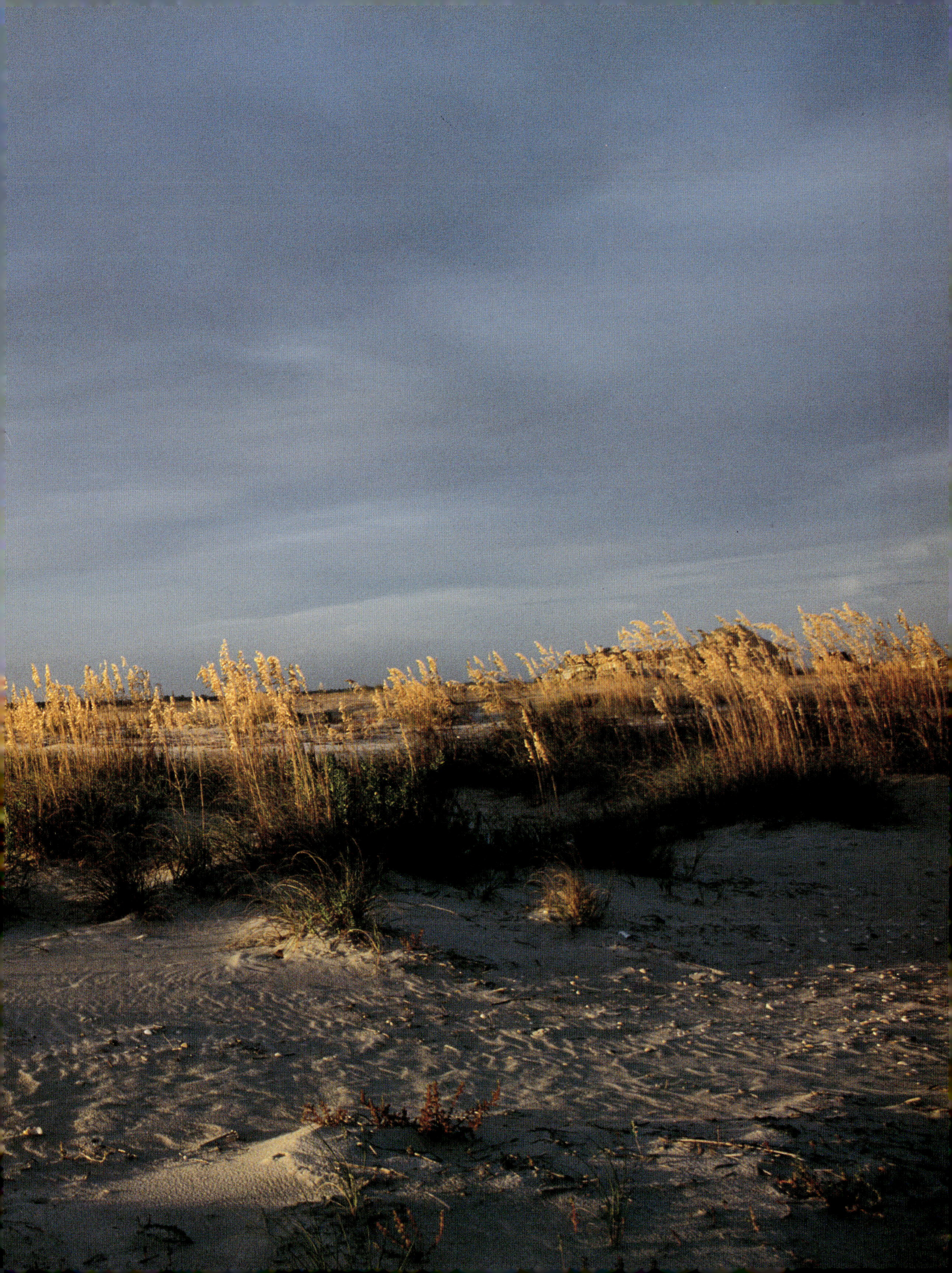

University of South Carolina, Columbia

Fall footwork at Furman University

Church Street and St. Philip's, Charleston

Wisteria in flower   *Overleaf*: Dawn from Caesar's Head

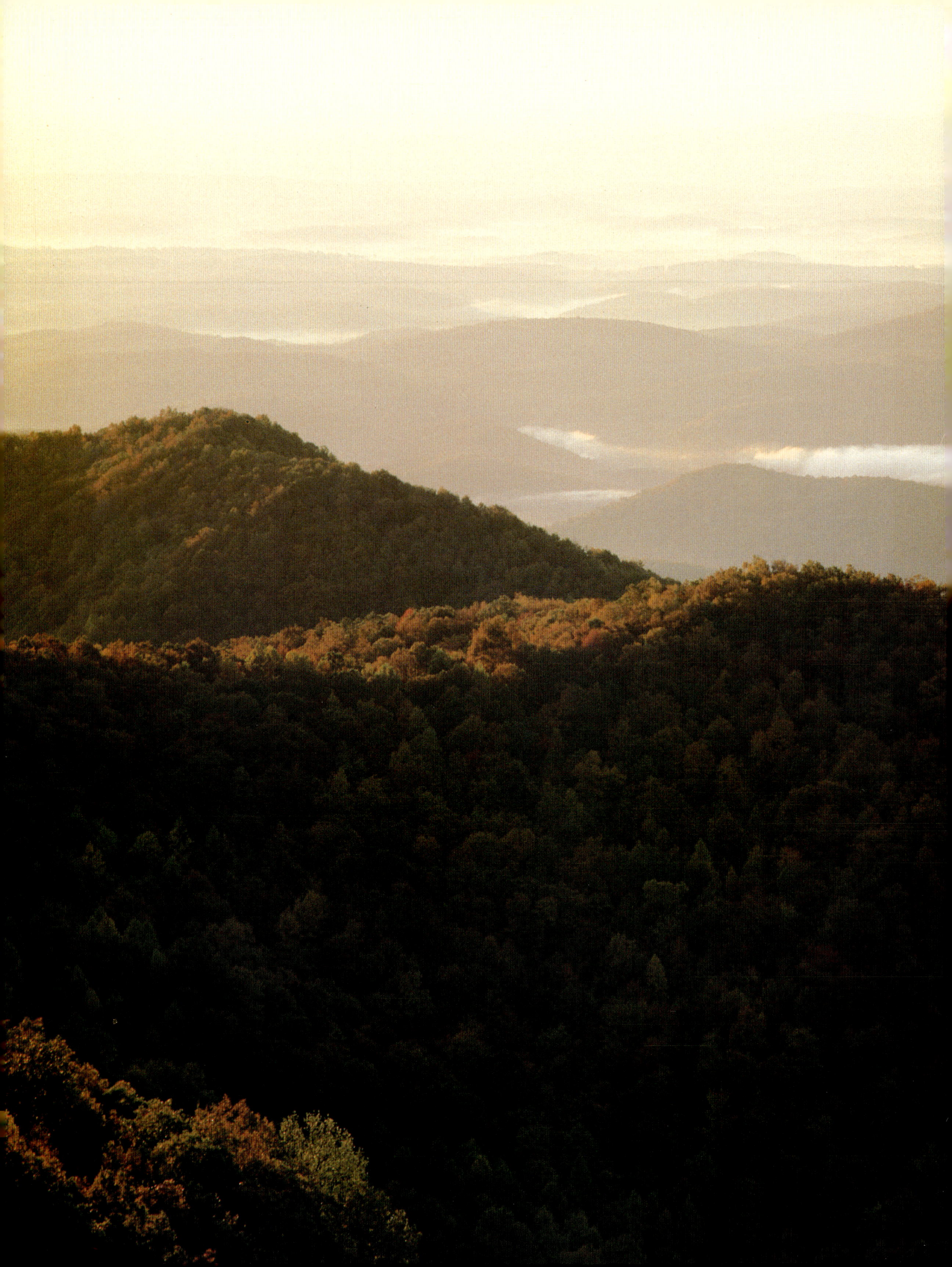

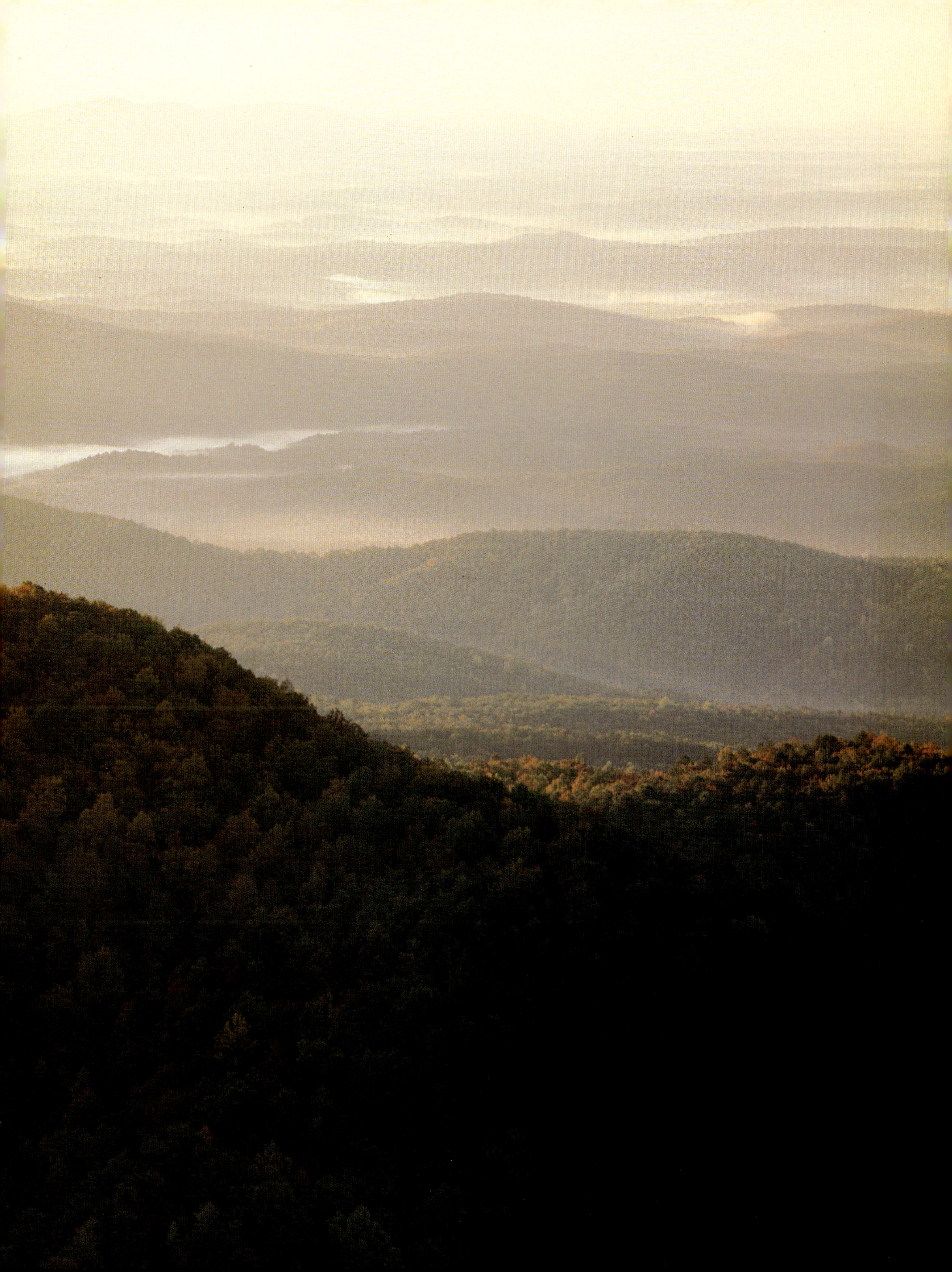

Shrimp trawler on intracoastal waterway near McClellanville

Terns take flight

Medway Plantation

The passionflower

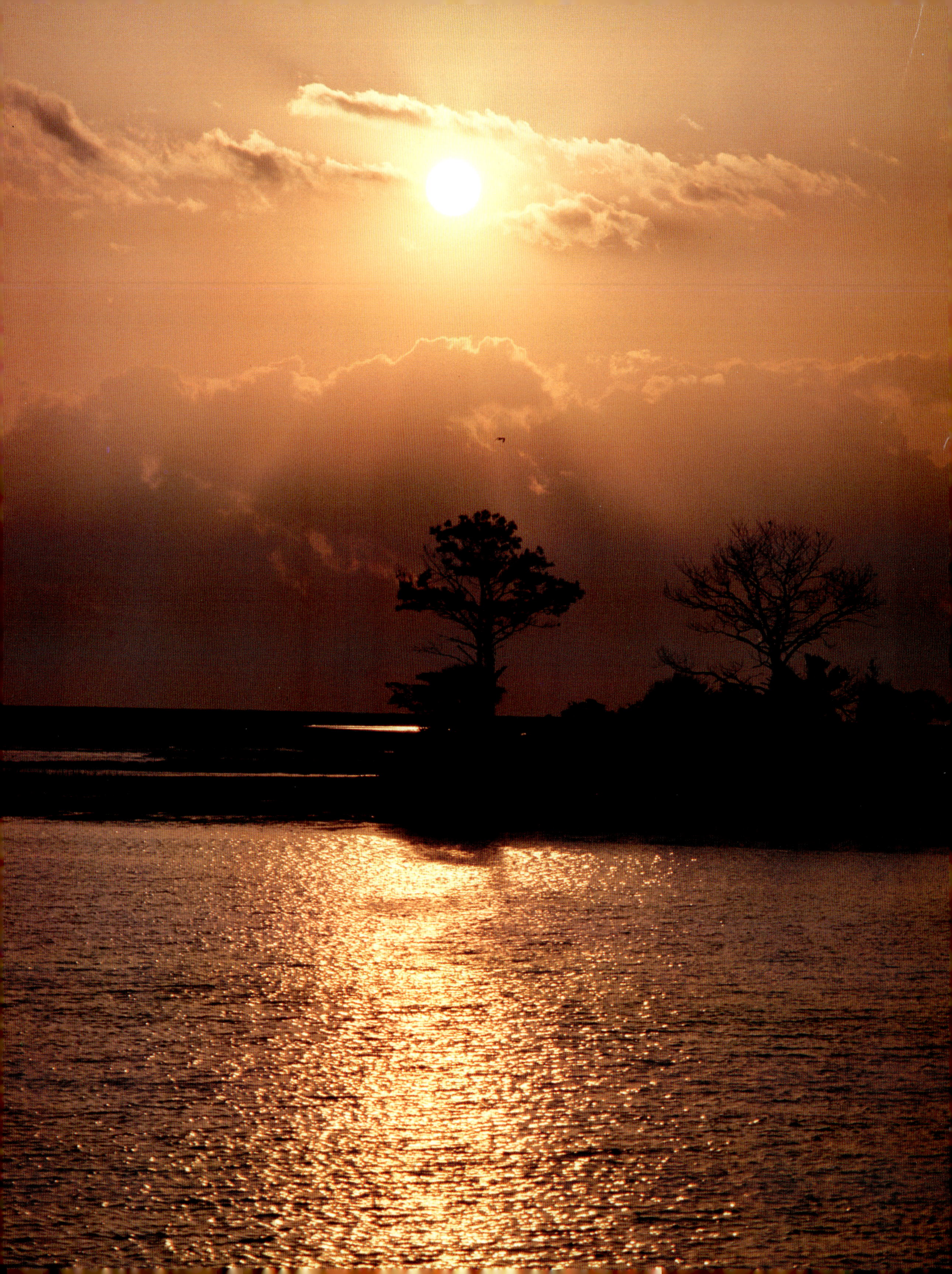

Dawn near Bull Island   View from Caesar's Head

39 Church Street, Charleston – 1743

Tourists before St. Michael's, Charleston   *Overleaf:* Shrimpboat with gulls at sunrise

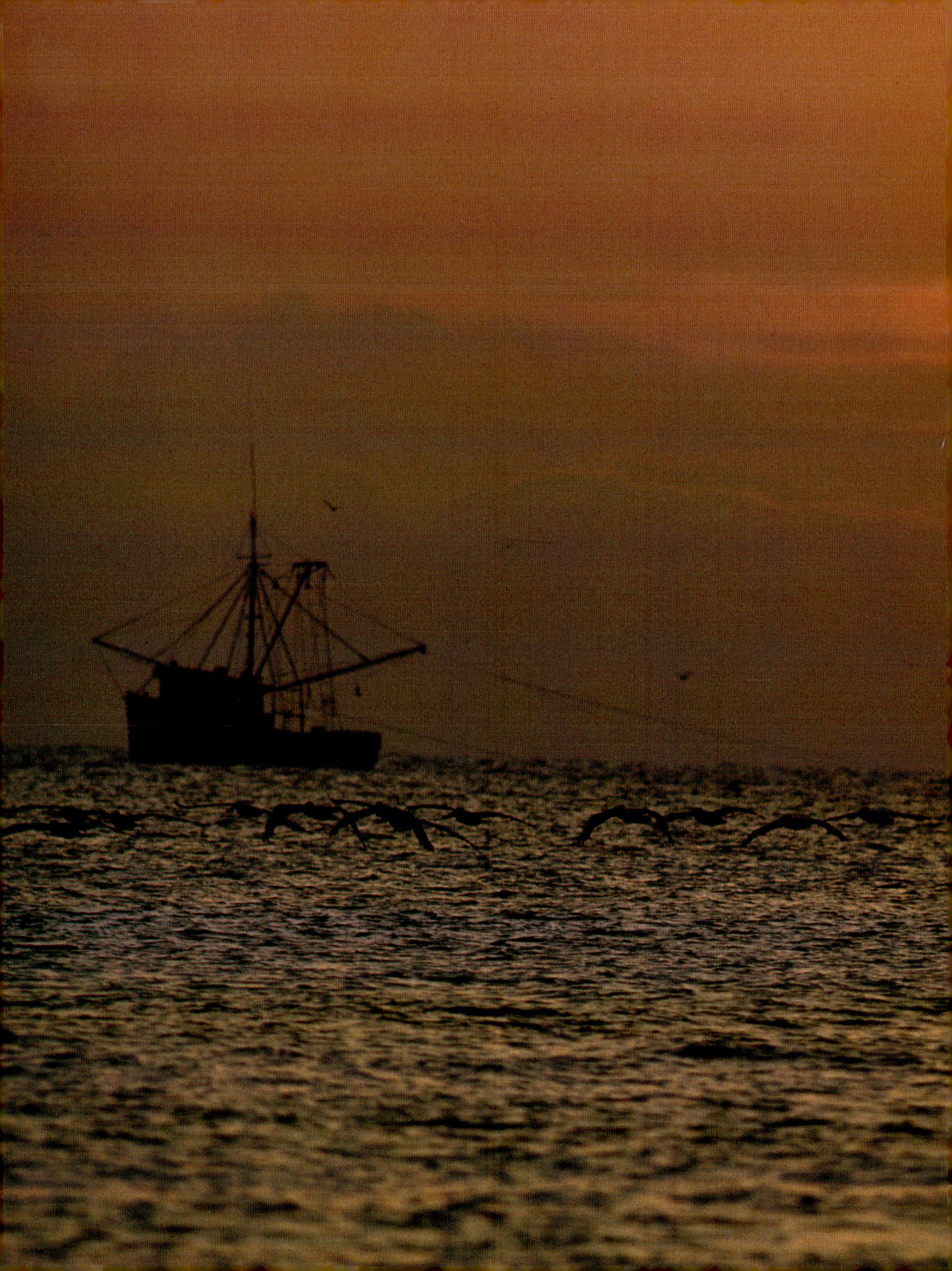

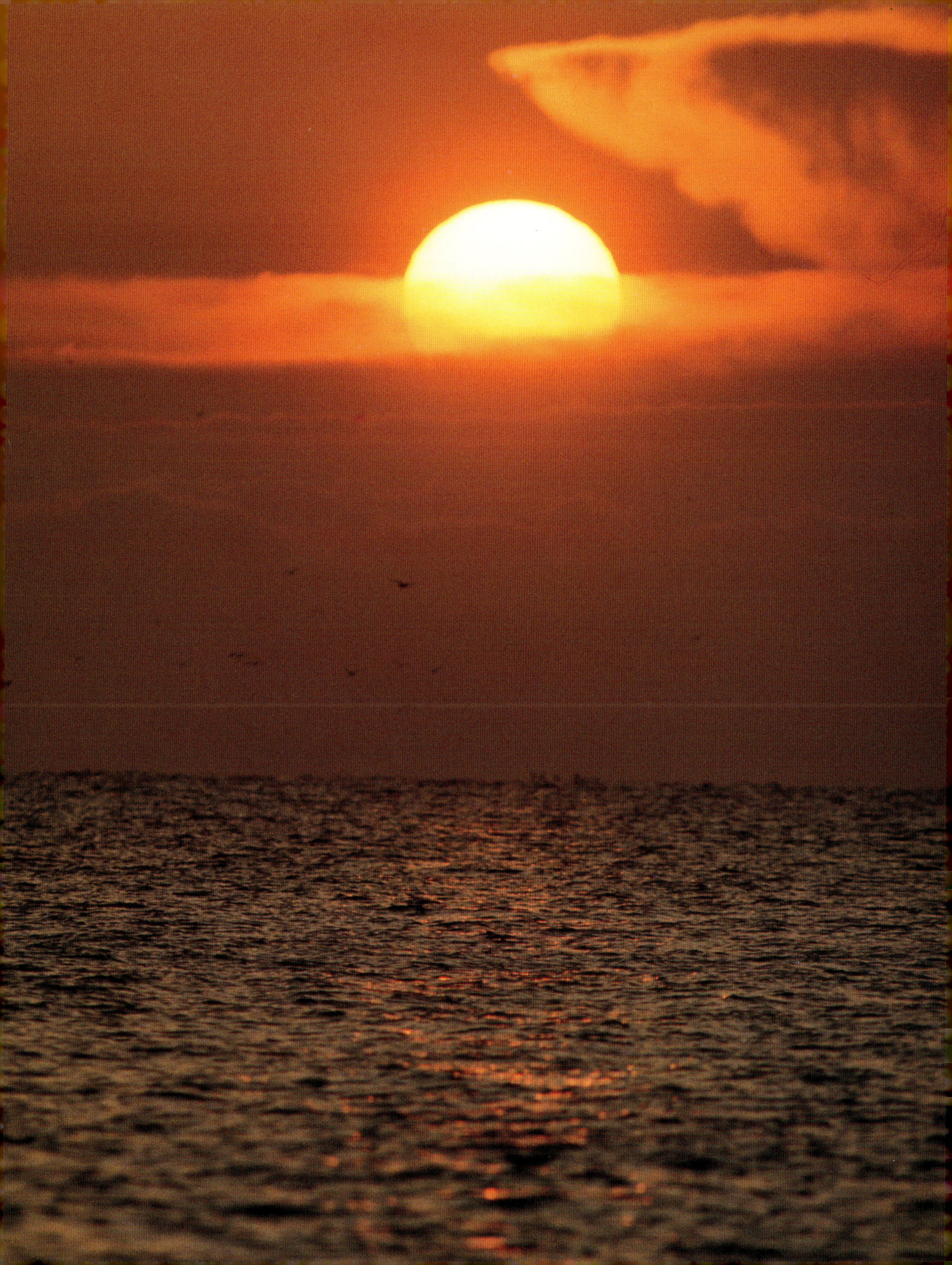

Ocean view from Dunes Club golf course, Myrtle Beach

Young egret at Boykin Mill Pond, Camden

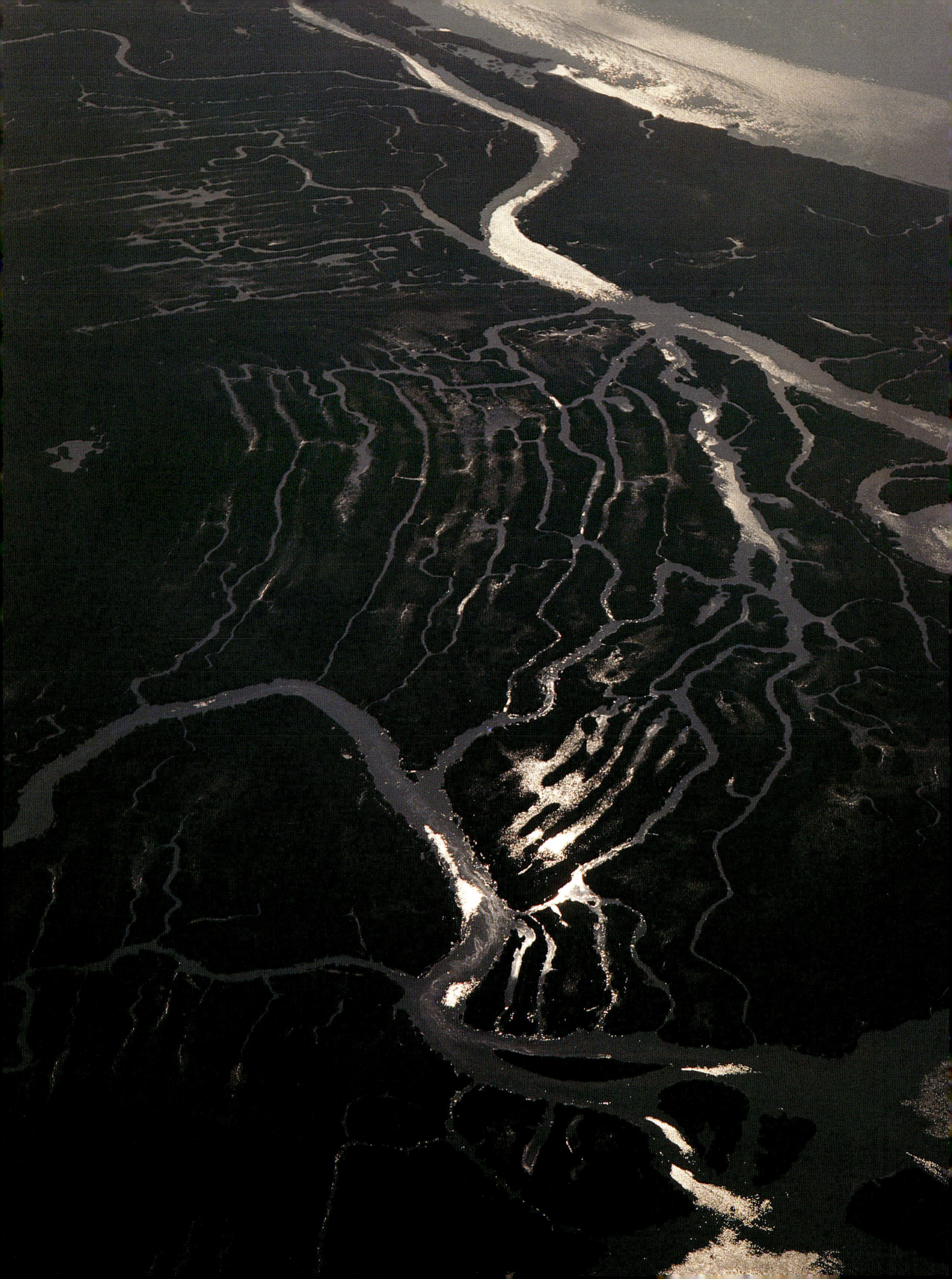

Marshland patterns along the Little Pee Dee River   Low tide on Broad Creek, Hilton Head Island

Fresh caught shrimp

Casting the net that catches the shrimp

Evelina Chisolm, Charleston

Charleston houses along The Battery   *Overleaf:* Kiawah Island sunrise

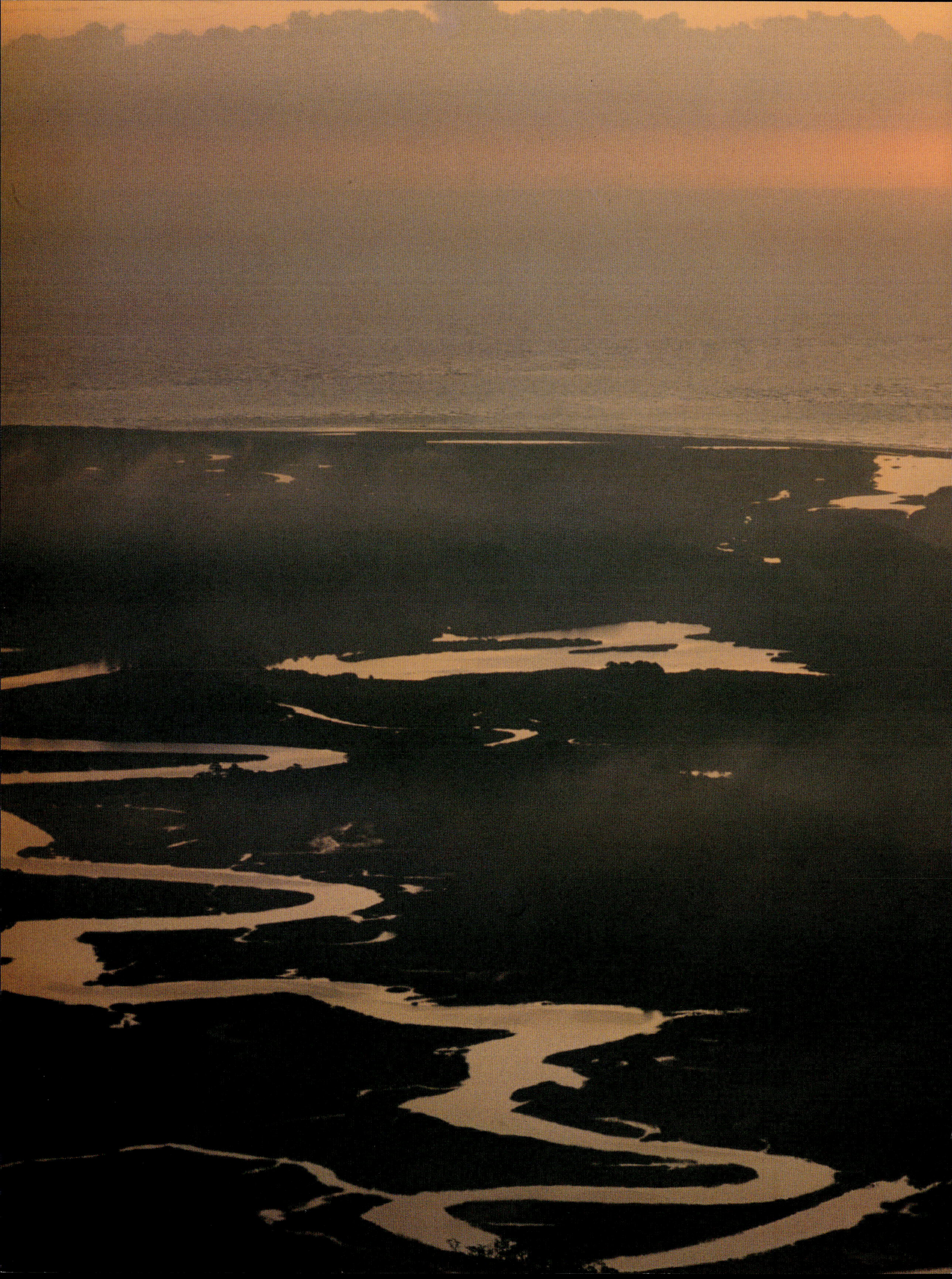

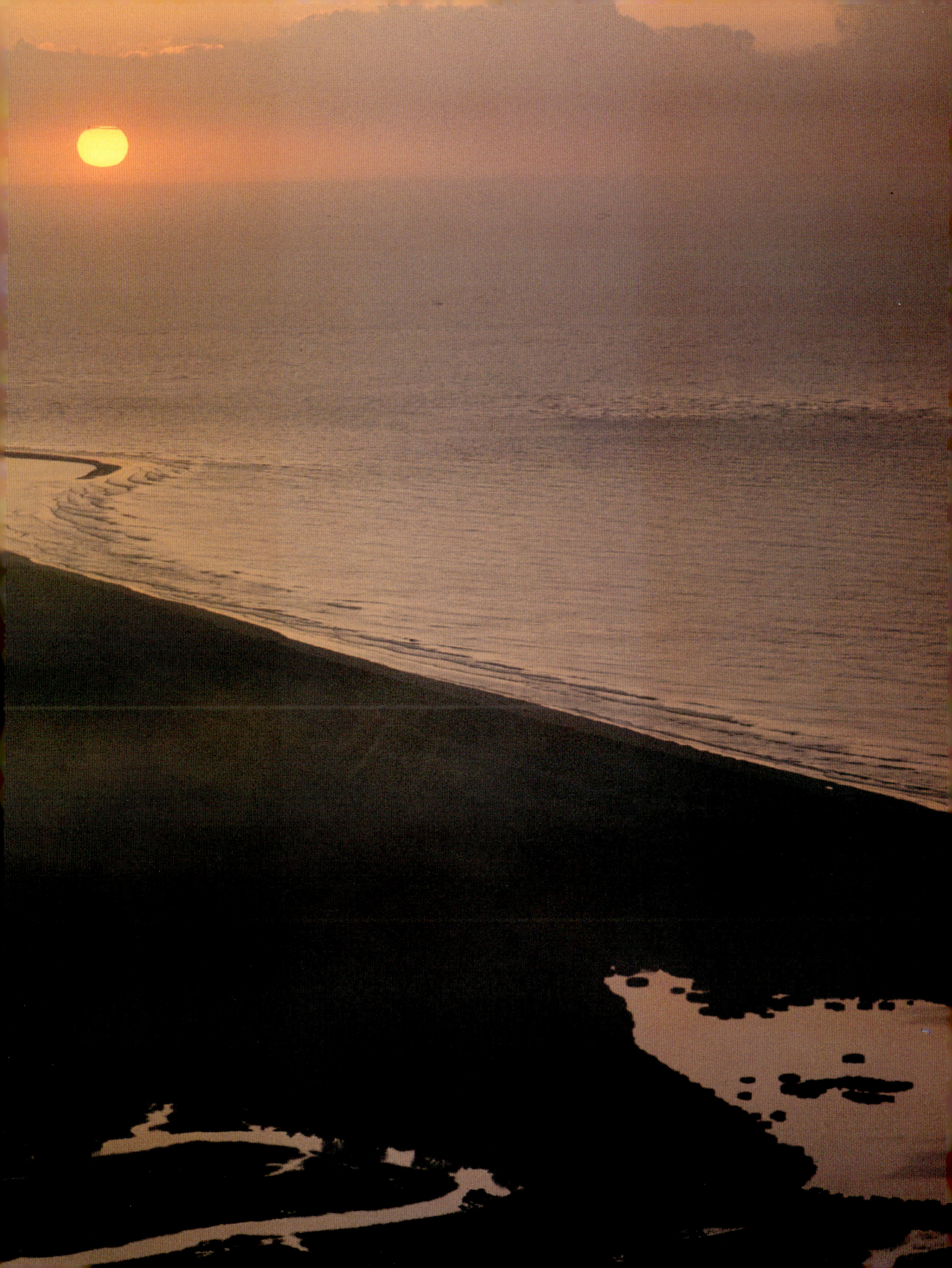

Egret is airborne from Pawley's Island

McClellanville piers and boats

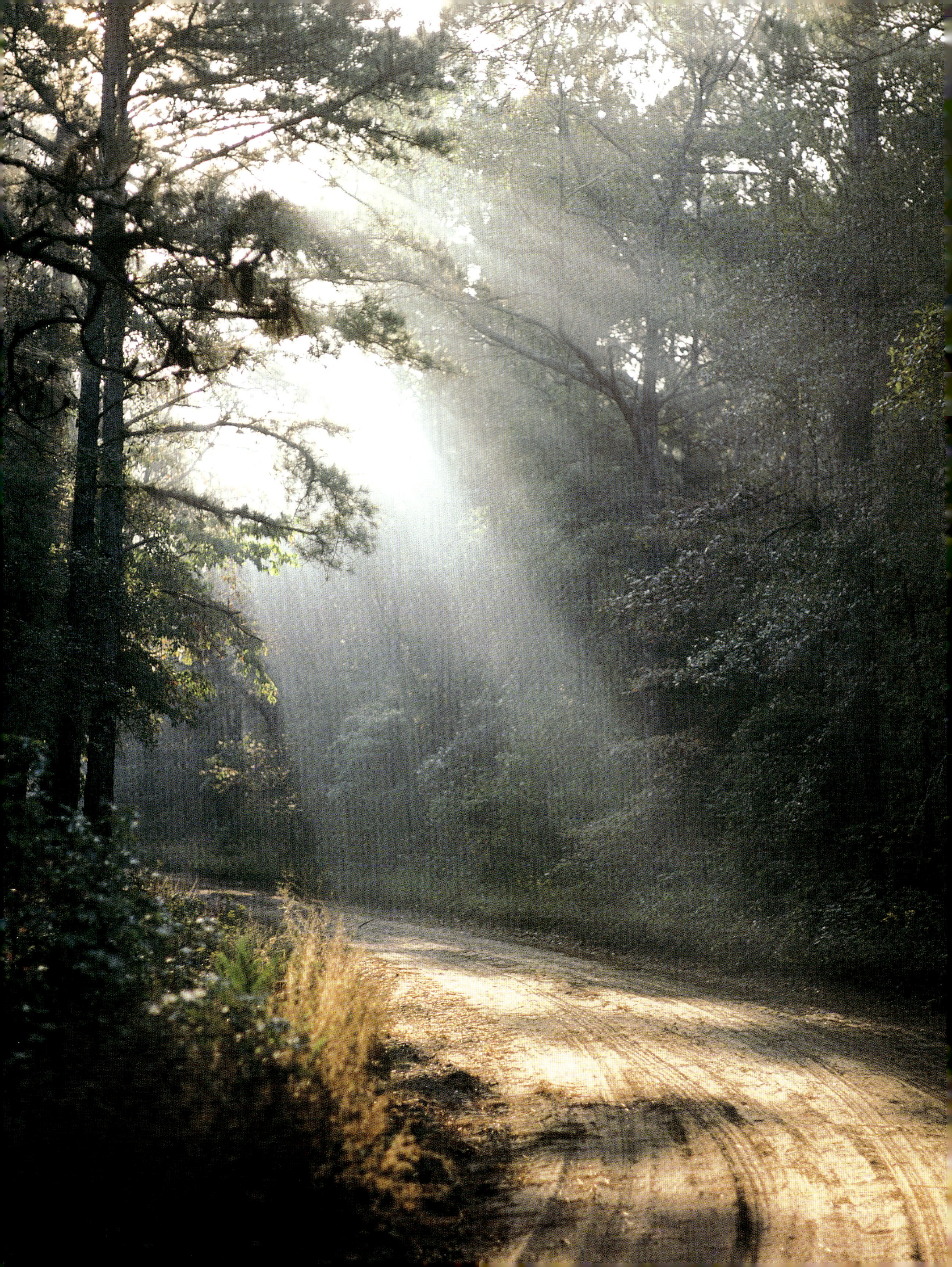

A bend in the road to Rosebank Plantation

Rocky Bottom store

Cattle egret

Cypress forest in Four Holes Swamp

Overleaf: Seabrook Island

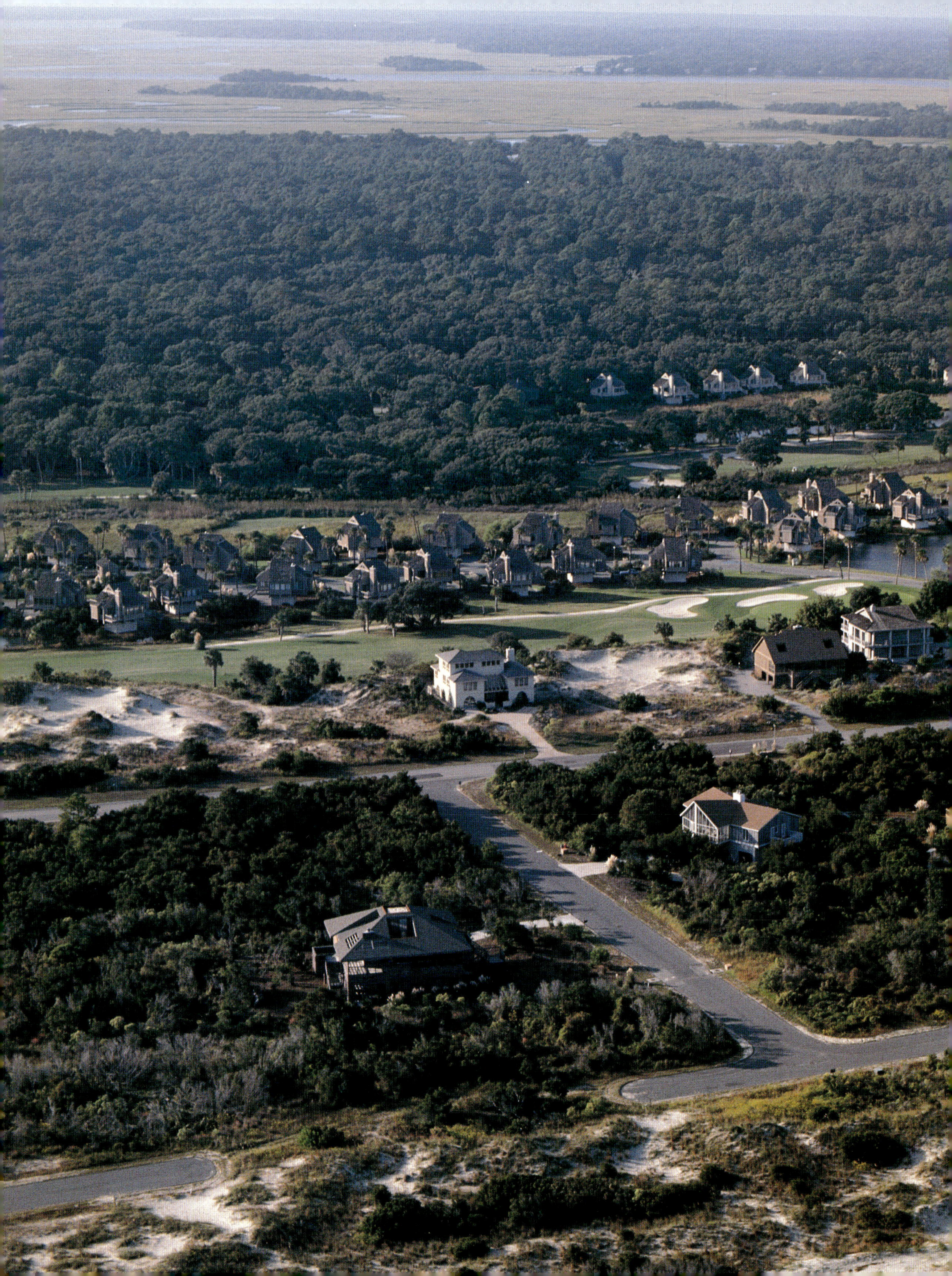

Magnolia Gardens